MODERN QUILT PERSPECTIVES

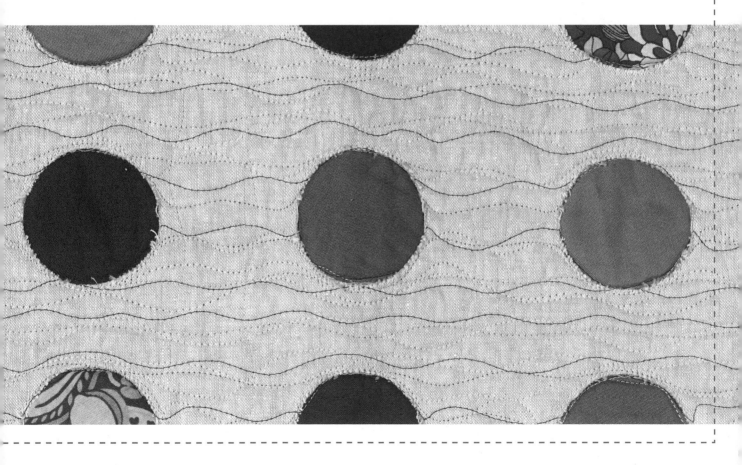

MODERN QUILT PERSPECTIVES

12 PATTERNS FOR MEANINGFUL QUILTS

THOMAS KNAUER

KP CRAFT
Cincinnati, Ohio

FOR MATILDA GRACE.

ALL THE
QUILTS
ARE FOR
YOU.

ACKNOWLEDGMENTS

I am so incredibly grateful for all the help I have had in bringing this book together; there are far too many people to list here, so I'll just try to hit the highlights.

Thanks to Andover Fabrics, FreeSpirit Fabric, Robert Kaufman Fabrics, Liberty Fabrics, Michael Miller Fabrics, Birch Fabrics and Moda Fabrics. It has been a privilege to work with your fabrics; your support has meant so much to me.

Thanks to Erin Sampson and Pellon for providing all of the batting for this book. Your support and encouragement has meant the world to me.

Thanks to Janome for your support and your sewing machines; both of those things made making this book and my quilts so much easier. I love your toys.

Thanks to Kelly Biscopink for bringing me to F+W Media, and to everyone at F+W for supporting this project and backing my ideas. And my profound thanks to Christine Doyle for her guidance and wisdom, and Julie Barnett for her vision and insight. I cannot thank the two of you enough for making what was in my head happen on paper. Books rule!

Thanks to Kate McKean for being such a super-agent! I totally need to make you a cape.

Thanks to Audrie Bidwell, Mary Kolb and Rachael Gander for jumping in and helping to get these quilts made. Without your support and stitches, this book would still be in progress.

Thanks to everyone who took part in making *Excess* and *Sum of Interrelations* happen; I wish I could list you all individually. You have no idea how much your support and excitement mean to me.

Thanks to Café Domenico and the Tramontane Café; without you I'd never get any writing done. And thanks to NPR and the Dead Kennedys; without you I'd never get any sewing done.

Thanks to Barry Gunderson and Kenyon College. What you taught me made this possible; I owe you more than you can imagine.

Thanks to Lisa Sipes. You, my dear, are a rock star. You make the quilts sing. You bring them to life. It is an honor and a privilege to work with you. I love your brain and the epicness it comes up with.

Thank you, Bee, for being so ridiculously awesome. I love that you love my quilts. I love that you are you. I am so proud to be your Papa.

Thank you, Babbit, for being born and for sleeping.

Finally, thank you, Katherine. Without your support and love, I'd probably be hiding in a corner, and without your editing, my words would likely be a confused noise. You are so far beyond extraordinary. I am blessed beyond words to have you in my life. I will always love you more and more and more.

CONTENTS

Foreword 8

Introduction. 10

Tools, Materials and Resources. 14

Techniques. 20

1 CONVERSATIONS 26

Ampersand. 28

Answer Key 34

Sum of Interrelations 40

2 IDENTITY 48

You Are Here 50

Mitosis. 56

Reunion 62

3 SOCIAL COMMENTARY 70

In Defense of Handmade 72

Palimpsest (Pride Flag) 80

Excess 86

4 THE QUILTING TRADITION 92

Timeline. 94

Split Personality 100

Cinderblock 106

Afterword 112

Templates. 116

Resources 124

Index 125

About the Author 127

FOREWORD

Walking through the first QuiltCon in February 2013, I stopped in my tracks when I came upon Thomas' quilt *In Defense of Handmade*. I'd heard people at the show talk about the quilt, so I knew the concept of it. But when I finally saw it (and admired and studied it), I realized the entire story of the quilt was right on the surface; I could not avoid it. The texture, the design, the words all conveyed the story of the quilt, and yet still, I wanted to know more and to see more. If you can look at a quilt and be interested enough to want to ask questions, then to me, it is a great quilt.

My own submission to the QuiltCon show, a quilt titled *Double Edged Love*, made me question myself. Who am I? Where did I come from? How did I get here? Where am I going? I had so many light-bulb moments going off in my head while I was making the quilt that I was sure no one else would understand or even like this quilt. But I felt myself growing with each seam I finished. At first, I was very protective of the story behind the quilt, but I found people were interested and wanted to hear more about it. Each quilt I make has a story, some of which are easier to tell and discover than others. But the story is the whole reason I make quilts.

As I chatted with Thomas one day, we talked about "modern" and what that currently means. He brought up a good point about figuring out what aesthetic matches the reality of today.

We make log cabin quilts, but we don't live in log cabins. Are we updating the past? Are we reviving an old design? Or are we working out our own sense of "today"? Maybe we are just capturing a moment, like in Thomas' quilt *URNH* (page 114), caught in a moment with his daughter. Or maybe we are both respecting and challenging our own history as "makers," like teenagers who have to question everything to figure out who they are and who they will become as grown-ups. Thomas believes those questions are very important in being "modern," and I do, too.

It seems to me that people pick up the needle and the DIY intent to be able to make a deeper connection to the things we have. Yes, we can buy cheap quilts and clothes, but to have made them ourselves, either from an easy pattern or a difficult one, is unique. We enjoy the choices required to make something, and we add a bit of ourselves along the way. Thomas is a master of adding himself to his quilts; he's a thinker, and his quilts demonstrate this naturally.

Perhaps "modern" means defining our space. Thomas questions our idea of space. How do we use it? How do we sleep in a bed, for instance? What's around us? What are the shapes and stories that make us who we are? How do you translate that into a quilt? We often hear about positive and negative space, but why is the space positive or negative and what does that do?

By adding layers of questions when we make our quilts, we promote a conversation. By making the quilts that we've committed ourselves to, with the decisions we've made and with our personal experiences added in, our quilts become a story, so much more meaningful than the quilt you buy at the local bargain big box.

Thomas encourages you to add your story, your life, your choices, your freedom to do what you choose. And when you do so, you will make something that is modern, unique and oh so special. Enjoy Thomas's thoughts in this book, be inspired and then go make your own story! And use it! As Thomas reminds us, "It is through use that quilts accumulate meaning and become a part of our lives."

Hear! Hear!

Victoria Findlay Wolfe

Victoria Findlay Wolfe
Author of *15 Minutes of Play*
Best in Show winner, *Double Edged Love*, QuiltCon, 2013

INTRODUCTION

I think of a quilt as bringing an idea to life, making that idea part of a home. The concepts embedded in the making of a quilt become part of someone's life, something they literally wrap themselves in. As such, quilts are somewhat unique objects, ones that are fundamentally interactive. Quilts provide warmth, comfort and protection; they can act as barriers or invitations; they can speak whispers or commands. Quilts have so many voices, elicit so many responses; they invite endless exploration and enforce no definitive rules.

To me, quilts are, first of all, cultural expressions—small statements about a time, a place, an idea. They speak about oneself and one's place in the world. For me, modern quilting—much like Modernism itself—is about transforming social, cultural and personal concerns into a quilting vocabulary and letting concepts drive formal explorations to produce truly resonant quilts. At the most basic level, Modernism and, even more so, Postmodernism are processes of perpetually critiquing assumptions and boundaries. Acknowledging that the world is complicated, these approaches consider experience through the lens of the cultural, rather than the absolute. Difference replaces superiority; dialogue supplants determination.

Historically speaking, Modernism came to prominence around World War I and Postmodernism during the 1970s. In each case, the public sphere began to accommodate an increasing number of voices; as communication technologies accelerated and spread, the

I HOPE THESE QUILTS WILL RESONATE WITH READERS AND BRING FORM TO CONCERNS AND PASSIONS THAT THEY MAY SHARE. BUT MORE THAN ANYTHING, I HOPE IT SERVES AS A STEPPING-OFF POINT FOR THOUSANDS OF NEW QUILTS, NEW VOICES AND NEW IDEAS.

number of voices compounded, and the possibility of singular truths diminished. As more voices emerged, communities embraced diversity and grew richer and more animated; greater complexity brought new combinations of thought and form.

In many ways, that's how the quilting world feels to me right now. I readily admit that I am kind of new to the community, but there seems to be a great deal of excitement in the industry at the moment. New audiences and practitioners are coming to quilting every day, looking to learn from experienced quilters even as they strive to find their own voices. The distinctions and differences between genres seem less important as diverse communities of quilters interact with heretofore impossible ease.

Within this diversity, no genre is better than another, no technique more important than another. Skill is important, but it is not the endpoint. Aesthetics matter but are simply a device for bringing form to an idea. This is not to say that everything is equal; sometimes things just don't work out very well, and critical discernment is still a valuable skill. It just means that each quilt ought to have, and be judged based on, its own internal logic, be considered on its own merits rather than some external set of norms or assumptions.

Over the past few years, terms like *traditional* and *modern* have been used in myriad ways, often placed in some sort of strange dichotomy. Assumptions abound as to what each of these terms means, but too often each seems to be reduced largely to stylistic

markers; the surface features take precedence over context and rationale.

This book is an attempt to sidestep that seeming opposition in favor of a perspective that embraces the vastness of possibility. All of these quilts began as a conceptual journey, taking inspiration from concerns personal and political, cultural and emotional. In many ways, every quilt is a starting over, a rethinking of assumptions to find the core of a concept and transform it into a quilting vocabulary. Each project represents a pairing of concept and form; each idea becomes more resonant through being embodied in a quilt and gains additional significance as it is incorporated into someone's home and life.

These quilts are all over the place conceptually and aesthetically, which only seems appropriate, as that very much reflects my life. This book, taken as a whole, attempts to express just how complicated, tragic and wonderful life is. It strives to bring voice to that reality and hopefully to inspire others to think deeply about their practice, to incorporate their lives into their quilts and then, more importantly, to incorporate their quilts into their lives. I hope these quilts will resonate with readers and bring form to concerns and passions that they may share. But more than anything, I hope it serves as a stepping-off point for thousands of new quilts, new voices and new ideas.

Finally, I hope this book opens doors for people outside the quilting community and offers a perspective that may bring new practitioners and audiences to a tradition I have come to love and respect.

BEYOND THESE QUILTS

Quilting is an extraordinary practice, born of a profound and significant history; it has perpetually responded to societal upheaval and aesthetic transformations. With the recent influx of new quilters, the community is again looking forward and asking where it might go. While I love all of the quilts in the book and am exceedingly proud of them, I fundamentally see them as a part of a much larger discussion, one that centers around the role that quilts play in our lives and how we might make quilts that meaningfully respond to the issues and concerns of our day.

More and more people come to quilting in search of a greater connection to the objects that inhabit their lives; many are searching for a more intimate relationship to their surroundings. Certainly style plays into this, but this impulse goes far beyond aesthetics; what an object says, what it is about, is of equal value as how it looks. As our connections expand to encompass the globe, many are seeking a groundedness in their personal environments: spaces and things they can relate to, not just possess. Quilting, along with a plethora of other crafts, is perfectly suited to fulfill these aspirations, as an extraordinary means to develop a voice and a space alike.

When I first started designing quilts, I was a little hesitant about actually doing patterns; I preferred to think of each quilt as a unique proposition, a singular event. Over time, though, as I began to better understand quilts, I came to a new understanding of the nature of patterns. They actually free a designer from the problem of the original object, the first or singular creation; in this way, quilting can be very much like printmaking. The pattern is only a map, a set of guideposts along the way to making a quilt. In many ways, a pattern is the quilt boiled down to its essentials, not just technically, but conceptually, and each remaking is an investigation of the ideas under consideration. I think of most of my patterns as a set of possibilities, the starting of a conversation about an issue, thought or world view. The specific

materials you choose and the ways you might vary the pattern are responses and replies. I often write somewhat loose instructions and, at times, design quilts that could be made in a thousand different ways while remaining true to the core of the project. I have come to really love the idea of quilt patterns, the idea of these quilts being made and remade in untold variations, and the ways in which these quilts will become parts of people's lives.

For these quilts, I have tried to use the simplest possible forms to get an idea across, not just to make the quilts accessible to the widest possible audience, but also to offer examples of how complex concepts and issues might be transformed into a relatively simple visual vocabulary. As quilting progresses into the twenty-first century, we have an opportunity to yet again rewrite the quilting lexicon, to reimagine the practice and its place in society at large. It is my profound hope that this book may, in some small way at least, contribute to that future.

TOOLS, MATERIALS AND RESOURCES

Pretty much every quilt starts with the same stuff: fabric, thread, tools for cutting and stitching. Then there is the rest of the stuff, the things that make everybody's space unique. What follows is a walk-through of the necessities and the tangents that make up my corner of the quilting universe, a glimpse that I hope is helpful in expanding your bit of the world.

USUAL STUFF YOU NEED TO MAKE A QUILT

Cutting mat: A good, self-healing cutting mat goes a long way. Get the size mat that will best fit your space and needs, but I swear by my 24" × 36" (61.0cm × 91.4cm) mat because I cut lots of big pieces of fabric.

Rotary cutter and blades: There are lots of styles of cutters with all kinds of fancy features; I use the most basic rotary cutter there is. The key, though, is to make sure to change the blade often to ensure clean cuts.

Pins: I have more pins than you can shake a pincushion at. I love the straight pins with colorful glass heads; they just make me happy and make me feel like sewing. I don't pin a lot of the time when I'm piecing, but when I do, I pin the dickens out of my quilts. I use safety pins for basting my quilts.

Hand sewing needles: I use all kinds of needles for my hand sewing, from fine sewing needles to embroidery needles to big old darning needles. I always do a few test stitches with different needles to see which needle feels right for the job.

Some of the stuff you'll need: clear ruler, large and small scissors, seam ripper, my very most favorite appliqué scissors (the ones with the weird blade), rotary cutter and extra blades.

More stuff: Glue stick, thread (colored threads for quilting and decorative stitches, white thread in bulk for piecing), safety pins for basting, fusible web, straight pins and a marking pen.

Machine sewing needles: I pretty much always use a standard, midweight needle; it works fabulously for most everything I do. Just like with my rotary blades, I make sure to change my needles often. Getting things just right is hard enough without the tools getting in the way.

Scissors: Confession: I am a scissors junkie. I have way more scissors than I need; I just love a pretty pair of scissors. That said, I recommend having a good pair of large fabric scissors, a good pair of small embroidery scissors and a crappy pair of craft scissors for cutting paper and templates and the like.

Glue stick: Simply said, glue sticks are incredibly useful. I use them for gluing down appliqué bits and

paper piecing; they're also great for making wee fabric collages with my daughter. I can't imagine not having a couple around.

Batting: It seems that everyone has their own preferences as far as batting, though there are certainly technical reasons to use a particular kind. I tend to like my quilts to crinkle a little less and to be light in weight so as to encourage sleeping under lots of quilts—though I frequently like my ultra-minimalist quilts to crinkle like crazy. As such, my favorites to work with are Pellon's Eco-Cotton and their Bamboo Blend. Of course, when working with Lisa we always discuss the batting options and make sure our choices suit the design and any technical issues that may arise.

Fusible web: I love Wonder Under. My mother introduced it to me when I did my first appliqué dress for Bee, and I am a creature of habit. I use fusible web for a lot of appliqué and reverse appliqué (except when I am lazy and just grab a glue stick from the pile in my sewing table drawer). As long as I use an appropriately lightweight web, I have not found any real effect on the drape or pliability of the finished quilt. There may or may not be rules on such things, but I am a big fan of using the tools that make a particular project the easiest to accomplish.

Thread: I buy a particular off-white cotton thread by the ton. I use it for everything. Good-quality thread is great to work with, and I think it is worth the bit of extra expense. Polyester thread is fine, for the most part, but years of training as a sculptor just insist that using cotton thread with natural fiber fabric makes sense and will survive the longest.

Machine feet: I use three feet for almost everything: my walking foot, my ¼" (6mm) foot and my clear appliqué foot. That walking foot is essential for quilting, and I always use it for sewing my bindings to the fronts of my quilt sandwiches. While I could just mark a ¼" (6mm) seam allowance with tape, I love the ease of a ¼" (6mm) foot. And that clear appliqué foot makes turning those tight appliqué corners so much easier. I never actually do free-motion quilting, but if you are so inclined, a darning foot is obviously important.

Marking pen or pencil: I have all kinds of marking devices, including chalk, water-soluble pencils and pens that disappear with the application of heat. I love the FriXion pens that disappear with the touch of an iron because they produce a smooth, fine line. I suggest trying a few marking tools to see what you like or what works best for a particular project.

Iron and ironing board: I love my iron. It was cheap, and it works like a dream. It doesn't leak water or cause any fuss. To me, that is the key to a good iron; if you can't say that about your iron, it is probably time for a new one. If you can, press on.

Seam ripper: Get several; you will always need them and will never be able to find one when you need one. In fact, stash one in every room you might sew in; having to look for a seam ripper just makes ripping seams all the more irritating.

Clear, gridded ruler: Your cutting ruler will be your best friend. I have several of different sizes for various tasks, but for the most part, I live by my 24" × 6" (61.0cm × 15.2cm) ruler; there is little it can't do.

Tape measure: I don't need it often, but it is right useful when it comes to finishing up a quilt. Keep a cloth tape measure in a drawer for squaring up your quilts.

REALLY HELPFUL TOOLS

A good wall: I have one wall in the studio that serves as a dedicated design wall for hanging designs in progress and laying out blocks. Design walls can be purchased or made with batting or fleece; either way, they are really useful. Walls are also good for banging one's head against when the inevitable frustration takes over.

A comfy chair: You are going to spend a lot of time at your sewing machine if you are quilting. A good, comfortable swivel chair with decent support is so incredibly nice to have. Your body will thank you.

Music or NPR: The silence of a sewing room can be deafening. I always have NPR or my archive of '70s and '80s punk to keep me company while working. I love my studio time, but it can get lonely.

Coffee or tea: Coffee is my bestest friend; well, my bestest inanimate friend.

A computer and Internet connection: Not only do quick Twitter breaks help me feel connected when locked in my studio, Google and YouTube provide those handy tips and technical reminders at a moment's notice. I also love sharing in-progress photos.

Sticky notes for reminders: Every quilt has those little details that get lost in my brain, so I jot them all down and stick the notes in places where I can't miss them. I used to use a notebook, but then I'd misplace the notebook. I also use a sticky note to jot down stitch length settings and the like for a project and stick it right on my sewing machine.

Credit card: Let's face it; you are going to need to buy fabric, and more fabric and more fabric. And sometimes the impulse will come in the middle of the night, so you are going to need a credit card. Try to not max it out.

Library card: Libraries are awesome, and they have lots of books about all kinds of stuff. When searching for inspiration, try the library.

Camera: Not only is a camera useful for taking pictures to share via social media, it can be really handy for taking pics of a quilt layout if you can't leave all the blocks and scraps out in between sewing sessions.

A room of one's own: A dedicated studio space is great if you have one; if not, find a way to make a temporary space yours. Also, go get a copy of Virginia Woolf's essay "A Room of One's Own;" it is one of the finest pieces of writing you will ever read and will likely speak to just about every quilter on the planet. Trust me. Read it.

The ever important ancillary stuff: sticky notes, books, a camera, lots of coffee and chocolate (for you, not me).

Whether you have a big stash or a small one, there is nothing quite like a stack of fabric waiting to become a quilt.

FABRIC

As both a fabric designer and a quilter, I think those perfect fabric choices are really important, but how "perfect" is defined depends entirely on the quilt or idea. Some quilts may require utterly exquisite fabric and flawless color coordination; others demand entirely random selections, the contrasts and contradictions enhancing both the ideas and the aesthetics. Either way, it is important to really consider just how the fabric and the fabric approach relate to the underlying goals of the quilt. This often means going beyond basic preferences and aesthetics and pushing one's boundaries. It also may entail using unexpected fabrics and materials. I am a big fan of corduroy quilts; I love their weight and heft. I also love mixing linens and cottons.

Certainly I am a fan of high-quality materials; local quilt shops and independent online retailers generally carry the best cloth. Such fabric will generally last longer and be easier to work with, but not everyone has that in their budget. In the end, what really matters is making the quilts no matter the materials you have.

RESOURCES

It is an amazing time to be a quilter because there are so many resources available to us via the Internet: video tutorials for almost any technique; access to almost any fabric one could imagine; a global community to offer suggestions, encouragement and help. I started quilting within the online community, and I truly consider that to be my quilting home. That said, the Internet is not the answer to everything.

In my practice, there are several places where I turn regularly for inspiration, advice and instruction.

Art history books: Obviously not everyone has shelves of art books on their walls, but libraries generally do. The Internet is nice for basic info, but nothing beats a book for really getting into a topic or for bouncing between ideas by randomly flipping pages.

When in doubt, write about it; drinking coffee and writing are truly essential to my quilting practice.

Getting to understand why people have made things can be as big an inspiration as what they make.

Museums: There is nothing like really looking at art. Whether you actually like a particular piece or not, spending some time up close, examining the details, can really help in finding those subtleties in an idea or a form. The more stuff one carefully looks at and considers, the more readily the ideas and inspiration will come.

Google and YouTube: I am pretty sure there is no quilting technique that cannot be found with a simple Google search. There is a lot to be learned from classes, and having other local quilters to learn from is great; if you have that, relish it. But there is nothing like YouTube for a quick technique refresher at two in the morning. In fact, I had a binding tutorial bookmarked for the entire first year I was quilting.

My local guild: Quilting can be very lonely. I exist primarily online, but I always look forward to my local guild meetings. It is a very traditional guild, and I am the only guy, but that doesn't matter in the least. Being with other quilters, listening to what they think about, seeing what they make and spending time with them serves as a reminder of the broader quilting community around us.

Social media: There is a vibrant quilting community online, and it is always there, thanks to those time differences between regions. Twitter, Facebook, Pinterest and Instagram really are wonderful places to find other quilters, share ideas and inspiration, and learn from one another.

Books and newspapers: I know I already mentioned my shelves of art history books, but to be honest, more of my inspiration comes from things I read rather than things I see. Whether it be a novel or *The New York Times*, what I read often sparks those initial ideas that I then craft into the final concepts and designs. Both reading and writing are extraordinary tools for refining ideas and garnering a clearer picture of the forms that will follow.

TECHNIQUES

Few, if any, of the quilts in this book use very complicated techniques. I am a big fan of using the simplest possible means to get an idea across, of letting the concept move to the foreground rather than be buried by technical wonders. That said, there are some basic techniques that all quilters need in their arsenal: matching seams, making half-square triangles, binding a quilt, etc. There are countless books out there that cover the basics of quilting in great depth, and there are myriad tutorials available on the Internet that do an excellent job of walking new quilters through just about any technical skill in a clear, step-by-step manner. For the quilts in this book that require unique techniques, I provide specific instruction with those quilts; for just about everything else, there is the Internet.

That said, I do have a few tips or hints that may be really helpful in making the quilts in this book.

CUTTING LONG STRIPS

Let's face it, cutting long strips of fabric can be a right bother. Anything longer than a folded bolt can lead to wiggles, as the folded layers shift relative to each other. To combat the wobbles, I make sure to use a fresh rotary blade and press the fabric after folding it for cutting. If I want really precise cuts, I use a bit of spray starch to make the fabric crisper. If you often get slightly *S*-shaped strips when you have to cut really long pieces, give these tricks a go.

1 Before cutting the strips, spray the fabric with a generous misting of starch, keeping the nozzle 8"–12" (20.3cm–30.5cm) away from the fabric.

2 Press the fabric with a dry iron to set the starch into the fabric fibers. When dry, cut your strips.

PIECING CURVES

Curves can be intimidating if you are new to them. There are two tricks to curves: lots of pins and practice. Using that many pins means I'm going to have to sew slowly, but I'm unlikely to zip through curves anyway.

I sew a couple of practice runs with a new curve, using scrap fabric or muslin before going on to the real thing. I also do at least one practice run if I haven't sewn a particular curve in a while. I probably ought to be more confident by now, but a little practice never hurts. Oh, and asking for help never hurts if the curved seam just doesn't want to come out right.

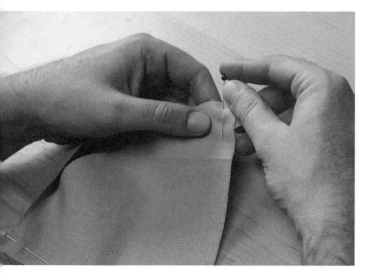

1 When getting ready to piece curves, start by pinning the fabric pieces right sides together, with the outer curved piece on top. Pin at the start of the curved seam and then at the end.

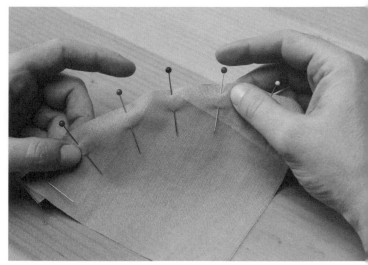

2 Next, pin at the center of the curve. From there, pin as often as every 1" (2.5cm) for a tight curve and make sure the fabric is evenly distributed between the pins.

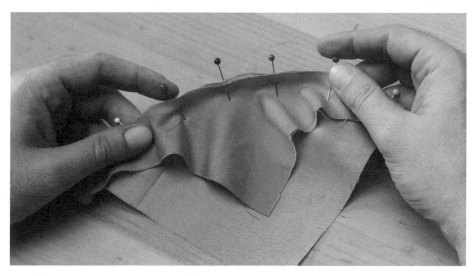

3 Flip the pinned pieces to the opposite side and you'll see that the fabric isn't laying flat. But it will once you sew the curved seam.

RAW-EDGE APPLIQUÉ

I absolutely love raw-edge appliqué. First off, it takes away the intimidation factor of doing complex appliqué and reverse appliqué, which is often the biggest barrier to taking on some amazing appliqué designs. Sometimes you just have to needle-turn a bit of appliqué, but otherwise I am a big fan of just cutting and going, letting the design rather than the technique lead the way. I also really love the soft, fluttery edge that raw-edge appliqué develops over time with repeated washes, that bit of softening that always reminds me that my quilts are meant to be used, not perfected.

1 Reverse your pattern so it appears in mirror image. Place the pattern on your surface, and place the paper-backed fusible web, fusible side down, on top of it. With a permanent marker, trace the pattern onto the paper.

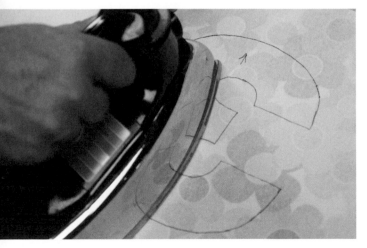

2 Place your fabric wrong side up on your ironing surface. Iron the fusible web onto the back side of the fabric, following the manufacturer's instructions.

3 Cut out the pattern and fabric with scissors. For raw-edge appliqué, cut on the pattern line. For needle-turn appliqué, cut approximately ¼" (6mm) outside the line.

4 Remove the paper backing from the fusible web, and place the appliqué shape right side up onto the background fabric. Fuse in place with an iron.

5 Sew around the appliqué shape just inside the edge of the fabric with a straight stitch or zigzag stitch. I prefer a straight stitch because it creates less of a visual divide between the fabrics.

SEAM ALLOWANCES

All of the quilts in this book use a ¼" (6mm) seam allowance unless otherwise specified. I know I already said this, but I love my ¼" (6mm) foot. Along with careful cutting, having a consistent seam allowance will make everything in life—or at least quilting—easier.

QUILT BACKS

I love quilt backs. As the father of two small children, I see the underside of a quilt almost as much as the top: quilts make such good bed-caves, tents and tumbling mats. Therefore, I put a lot of consideration into just how I put my backs together.

I generally prefer doing pieced backs, bringing bits of fabric from the front of the quilt into the design of the back, even if it's only a few scraps. I think of the front and back as in conversation with each other, engaged in a sort of call and response.

I'll temper a complicated or vivid top with a sedate back, giving the top the space to stand out. With more minimal tops, I frequently consider the back as a place to go wild, again marking out a contrast, one

With a ¼" (6mm) foot, all you need to do is line up the edge of the foot with the edge of the fabric. A perfect ¼" (6mm) seam!

that is perhaps felt rather than seen. Backs like these are perhaps my favorites; I always know that just below that seemingly simple surface is an explosion of color and pattern. I also design my backs in anticipation of the quilting to come: with a busy top, the quilting hides within the overall design, so a simple back allows that quilting to be a revelation when the quilt is flipped over.

QUILT LABELS

I did not label my first quilts, and those actually remain unlabeled. But I had a revelation awhile back that changed how I regard quilt labeling. The practice does not seem to be so much about attribution as

archeology: quilt labels begin the long string of interconnections that will occur during the life of a quilt.

Many of the quilts for this book were pieced by friends and collaborators, and all but one was quilted by Lisa Sipes; so my labels reflect that. This is partly a matter of proper attribution, but more importantly, it reflects the relationships that were involved in each quilt's making. The labels speak to the community in which I work; they give a date, which places each quilt into the context of my life. For me, the specific information on the label is less important than the context it provides, the way it starts the story of any particular quilt and brings that story into the larger collective of quilts and quilters.

I have a general label onto which I write the information, and I also print out specific labels for particular quilts, especially collaborative or bee quilts. And because I almost always do pieced backs, I piece those labels right into my quilt back before the quilting; making the label a permanent part of the quilt has both practical and poetic value.

QUILTING

Designing and piecing a quilt is only half the battle; getting the piecing and the quilting to truly work together is a whole other level in making a quilt. For all of the quilts in this book, I was blessed to be able to work with a truly extraordinary quilter: Lisa Sipes. Although it is obvious that Lisa's technique is impeccable, what really makes her work exceptional is the thought that goes into her quilting. She does not simply respond to the forms, looking for ways to fill the spaces; instead, Lisa spends time with the idea of the quilt, reflects upon its intent and looks for ways to enhance or expand its meaning.

Of course, the aesthetics matter; quilting ought to add to a quilt formally as well as figuratively. Lisa and I engaged the quilting for this book as an architectural process, building up a quilting plan for each quilt, regarding each element and space on its own terms in order to find meaningful responses to the original design. At times, the quilting needed to recede, to avoid interfering with the design; in other cases, the quilting stepped forward to entirely rewrite the quilt. To me, this is the essence of quilting: in stitching the layers together, it effects the final transformation of the quilt. To give an analogy, the pieced top is akin to a screenplay, and the quilting transforms it into the finished film, readying it for its ultimate realization on screen, or in the case of a quilt, for binding and a long life in someone's home.

Obviously not everyone has access to someone like Lisa, or even the desire to have their quilts finished by a longarm quilter. What matters to me is the thought that goes into the quilting, the fitting of the quilting and piecing together conceptually as well as formally.

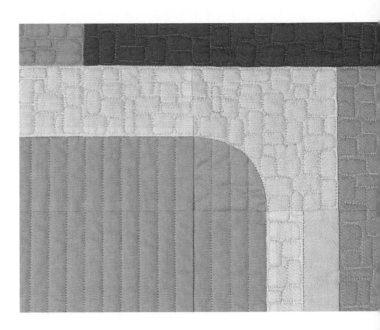

It is the meaningful integration of all the elements, their ultimate marriage, that produces a truly resonant quilt. The quilting itself may be enormously complex or remarkably simple; what matters is the harmony formed in the final execution of the quilt.

BINDING

I generally cut my binding strips 2½" (6.4cm) wide because I like a generous binding that serves as a wee border, but I will vary that width depending on the batting decisions for each quilt. If I go with a lightweight, low-loft batting and dense quilting, I cut 2" (5.1cm) wide strips. When I double-layer the batting or I tie the quilt, I go with the wider strips to give myself a bit more room to maneuver.

RELAX

I love perfection, but in the end, it is the practice of making the quilt and the relationship you have with it afterward that really matter. I do everything I can to get things to match up just so, especially for the quilts in this book, but I do not let my inexperience get in the way. Technical skills improve by making more quilts, so don't let the process get in the way of the practice.

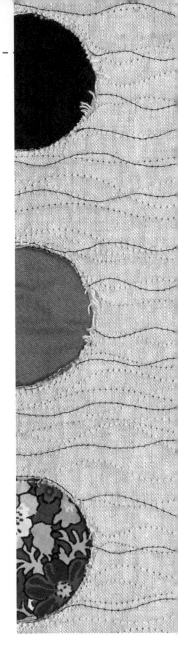

I am of a new generation of quilters who did not come to quilting through a relative, friend or, indeed, anyone with whom I had an immediate local connection. My community is first and foremost global; my conversations occur on the Internet through various technologies. Most of my lessons have come from YouTube or other online tutorials. This virtuality, though, does not make my relationships any less real; we share our creative and personal lives as we learn from each other and exchange the things we make. As such, the core practice of quilting has changed very little over the centuries.

Whether it be a local gathering working on a communal quilt a century ago, a modern Internet community swapping blocks across the globe or a simple, yet profound, personal act of giving a quilt to another person, quilts are as much about how we spend our lives together as they are about themselves as objects. Quilts provide a reason to come together while producing something of practical value. Indeed, both aspects of quilting—the coming together and the finished quilt—are of essential value to the community at large. Quilting produces its own circular logic: a community produces quilts, which in turn create community. As such, it is easy to speculate that the recent revival of quilting stems from just this impulse—the desire to be and work together, to be part of a larger conversation, to be connected.

Each of the quilts in this section explores different ideas of and approaches to quilting conversations. Whether it be a collaboration on a common project or an investigation of the ways in which a quilt can bring people together, these quilts celebrate the practice of quilting as a locus for meaningful engagement, as a prompt for communication and understanding. In this way, I am fundamentally looking at quilting as a touchstone for understanding and creating the communities in which we want to participate and, by extension, the world in which we hope to live.

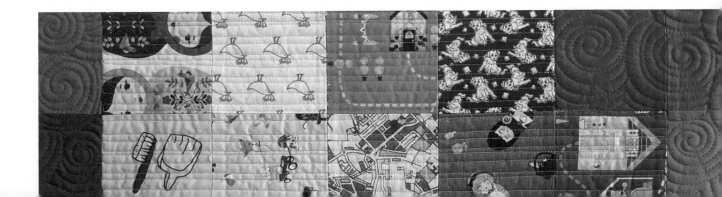

AMPERSAND

At first blush, *Ampersand* (the symbol for the word *and*) seems a fairly simple quilt, conceptually speaking; it is a storytelling quilt, a sort of choose your own adventure. My daughter and I snuggle under the quilt, pick one of the illustrated prints, a pirate perhaps, and begin a story. When we need fresh inspiration, one of us says "and," points to another of many prints within the ampersand itself, and the story continues. This process can go on for hours.

That is the one side of *and*. It strings thoughts and things together, letting more and more happen; it is the way the action unfolds. In this way, *and* is fundamentally optimistic; it assumes the story will not, in fact, end. As a simple conjunction, it anticipates the next action, idea or object; for a split second, what will follow the word *and* is uncertain, a moment of infinite possibility. For my daughter and me, it can be a moment of pure joy as we wonder just what might happen next. That is the word *and* as seen through the details, those little steps and decisions that make up a life.

At the same time, *and* can take on a very different tone when it becomes a question, one that brings a near-existential weight of expectation along with it. "And now what?" may well be the most haunting question I have ever known. That omnipresent "And?" perpetually looms large; it interrogates me, expects more from me. Nothing is ever enough for that ampersand; it is the voice in the back of my head that wonders if I have done enough.

This is the fundamental duality of this quilt; it is a balancing act of possibility and expectation. With my daughter, I get lost in the interplays of possibility within the ampersand, the myriad variations that make up the wonder of life. Alone, seeing the ampersand in its totality, I recall my own self-doubt and wonder what's next. *Ampersand* is a quilt of two stories: one that creates itself out of the endless details, the other formed of the vast totality. The perpetual question is, which story are you in?

FINISHED SIZE

85" × 85" (215.9cm × 215.9cm)

MATERIALS LIST

- 1 yard (1m) each of 6 tonally related solids. I used 6 different Kona blues, but this can be done in any color set. Try to keep the colors close, but not so close that they all look the same.

- 225 squares of fussy-cut illustrated prints: 3½" × 3½" (8.9cm × 8.9cm)

- 5 yards (4.6m) fabric for backing

- ½ yard (0.5m) fabric for binding

- The usual stuff you need to make a quilt (see page 14)

NOTE: Go crazy and include all kinds of stuff for the prints. The more variety, the better. Doing a print swap is a great way to get enough prints to really pull this one off. With 225, you will have a few extra, but I always like a few spares at hand just in case.

CUTTING INSTRUCTIONS

Cut each of your solids into 3½" × 3½" (8.9cm × 8.9cm) squares. You should be able to get 120 squares from each yard (1.0m), which will give you a few extra to play with as you lay out the quilt.

PIECING

Piece the top first in 9 groups of 100 squares. Then sew those groups together. This is really a straightforward quilt; what matters is the overall design. Do not stress over which solid goes where; random works best. Diagram 1.

FINISHING THE QUILT

After your top is completed, layer your backing right side down, your batting and the quilt top right side up. Baste the layers together, and then quilt as desired. For this quilt, Lisa and I decided on swirls for the field of blue—eddies and pools of mystery—and rhythmic straight-line quilting for the ampersand itself.

Bind using your preferred method.

TONAL VARIATION

I absolutely love using multiple tones of a color pieced together in places where a single color would normally suffice. It lends such a rich range of tones to a quilt; it subtly disrupts the idea of a background by allowing the different tones to move backward and forward in relation to each other; and it produces diverse interactions with a single quilting thread color. It also fills large spaces with all kinds of wonderful geometries. Consider using traditional or improv blocks in closely related tones in places where you might normally use a single swath of solid.

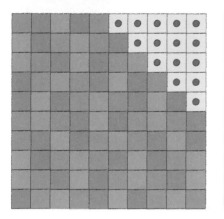
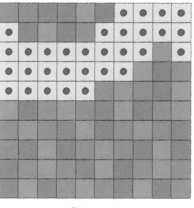
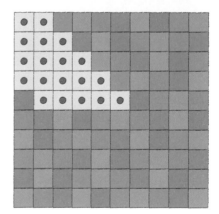

Diagram 1

STORIES

In my life, quilts and stories just go together. Whether
it is curling up alone on the couch with some dense
philosophy, reading a novel out loud with my wife or
making up endless stories with Bee, quilts are always
involved. Quilts and books just go together, along
with a cup of tea (or coffee or hot cocoa). It isn't just
the fact that quilts are cozy; every quilt tells the story
of its making, each stitch and fabric choice a reminder
of its maker. The coming together of quilts and stories
(printed or invented) never ceases to make me happy.

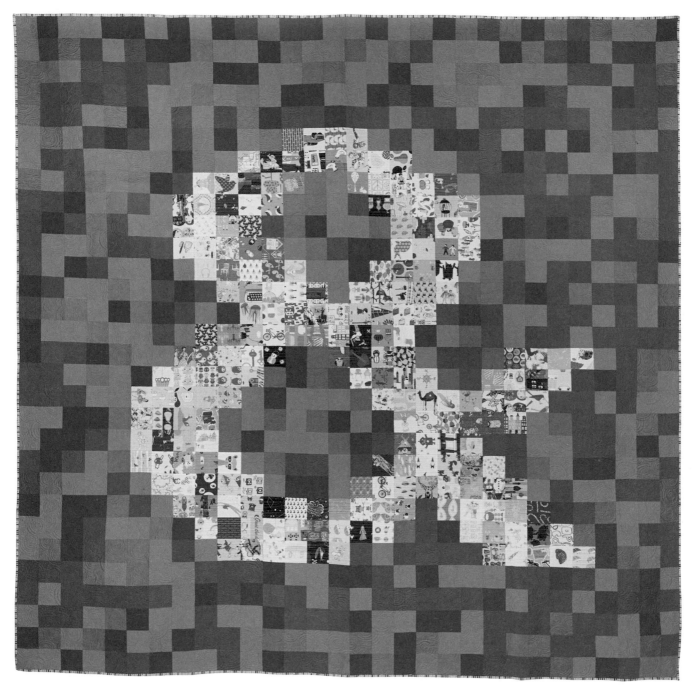

Credit: This top was pieced by Rachael Gander.

ANSWER KEY

As both a student and a teacher, I have long dreaded the standardized test; to this day, the very idea of ever so carefully filling in those dots with a number-two pencil makes me slightly twitchy. The second those forms hit my desk, I knew all subtlety was doomed, that thought would be forced into neat little circles; repetition and recitation would replace exploration and discussion. In the process of darkening one circle or another, context would give way to the absolute, that one right (or right enough) answer.

Answer Key is something of a thought experiment for me, a way of critiquing the entire logic of the multiple-choice test. What if we were to make all of our conversations like those tests? Imagine dinner with your kids or a Thanksgiving feast that had to be fit into the logic of those dreadful dots. *Answer Key* as a table runner makes just that inquiry. Its dots are already neatly filled in; the questions have been asked and answered; conversation has, at least hypothetically, been reduced to the simplest possible bits of information. Such a meal would be dreadful, much like all those tests we took in school.

As a thought experiment, *Answer Key* is a reminder of the wonder in the details, the pleasure of just sitting around the table and talking. The questions and answers are merely the starting points; the true connections between people happen in the tangents, in the spaces between the answers, between the dots. *Answer Key* exhorts us to follow the overlapping threads that intertwine to produce the profound texture of our lives together.

28" × 54" (71.1cm × 137.2cm)

MATERIALS LIST

- 1½ yards (1.4m) neutral linen blend (I like Essex linen)

- ⅛ yard (0.1m) each of 4 different shades of gray

- 14 squares 3" × 3" (7.6cm × 7.6cm) of various bright and colorful prints

- 1¾ yards (1.6m) fabric for backing

- ⅓ yard (0.3m) fabric for binding

- The usual stuff you need to make a quilt (see page 14)

NOTE: If you are using a light shade of linen blend, you may want to ensure that the prints and grays won't show through in the seam allowance. If they do, you can fuse a lightweight interfacing to the back of the linen before getting started.

CUTTING INSTRUCTIONS

Cut the linen fabric to 24" × 52½" (61.0cm × 133.4cm).

Cut 14 squares 3" × 3" (7.6cm × 7.6cm) from each gray fabric.

PREPARING THE LINEN

You will be cutting seventy 2" (5.1cm) circles from the linen top along a grid. To do this, you need a ruler, a removable marking pencil or marker, and a 2" (5.1cm) circle to trace.

First draw a line down the center of the linen lengthways. Then draw lines 4¼" (10.8cm) and 8½" (21.6cm) to the left of that center line. Repeat on the right side of the line.

Next draw a line horizontally across the linen 3½" (8.9cm) from the bottom. Draw lines every 3½" (8.9cm) above the first until you have 14 horizontal lines. The top line should be 3½" (8.9cm) from the top. Diagram 1.

Finally, center your circle template at each intersection on the grid and trace the circle. You should have 70 circles traced.

Now carefully cut out each circle with scissors. This is the quilt top.

Follow the instructions for your preferred marking pen or pencil and remove the lines to ensure your guide grid does not set into the fabric.

Diagram 1

THE JOYS OF REVERSE APPLIQUÉ

I am a big fan of reverse appliqué. Actually I've yet to meet a way of doing appliqué that I didn't like, but reverse appliqué gives such a different feel that I always find myself looking for reasons to incorporate it into a project. By setting the appliqué pieces behind the top surface of the quilt, it inverts the usual foreground/background relationship, which produces subtle optical complications, pulling the viewer into the quilt rather than drawing the eye to elements placed upon the surface.

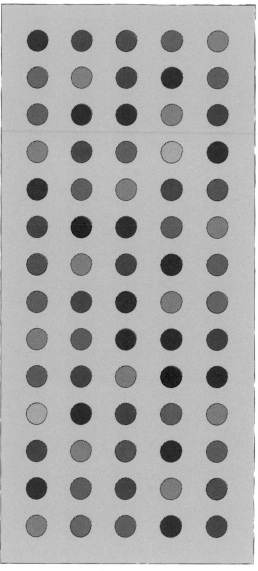

Diagram 2

PIECING THE TOP

Apply glue from a glue stick to the outer edges of the print squares and glue your print squares behind one circle in each row; random is best. Make sure the prints are facing up. Use your preferred method to sew the squares in place for this reverse appliqué. I like a simple straight stitch just off the edge of the circle, but a tight zigzag is fine as well.

Repeat this process for the gray squares, making sure there is only one of each shade of gray per row. Diagram 2.

FINISHING THE QUILT

After your top is completed, layer your backing right side down, your batting and the quilt top right side up. Baste the layers together, and then quilt as desired. For this quilt, Lisa and I chose a fluid approach to the quilting, allowing the lines to flow around the rigid dots of the answer key, like water around stones in a stream.

Bind using your preferred method.

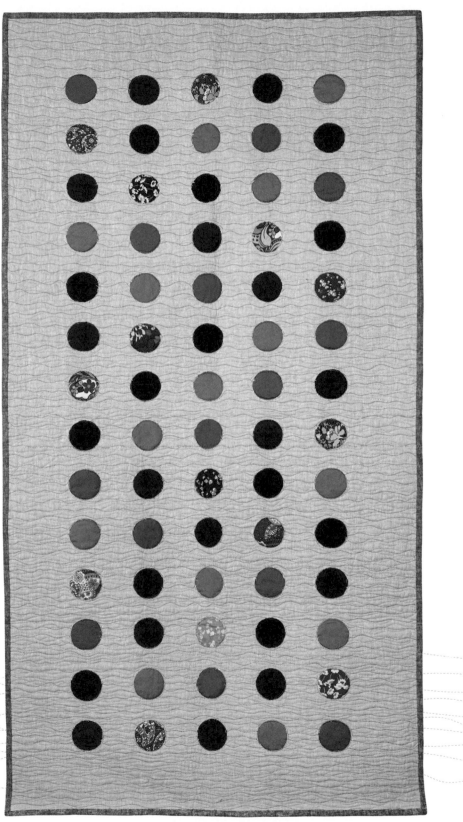

Credit: This top was pieced by Mary Kolb.

SUM OF INTERRELATIONS

So much of my quilting life is wrapped up in the quilting community itself, those relationships both personal and professional that occupy and add meaning to my life. Of course, this has long been a significant element of the quilting tradition: bees and guilds abound. One of the amazing things about the current quilting community is the way that online activities have expanded the reach and potential for those relationships.

As I was thinking about this quilt, I kept returning to the ways in which individuals simultaneously exist within and form communities. It is a relationship far more complex than simply joining a group; each new member reforms that group and is in turn reshaped by it. And that thinking, of course, sent me back to my books, where I found this line from Karl Marx underlined:

"SOCIETY DOES NOT CONSIST OF INDIVIDUALS BUT EXPRESSES THE SUM OF INTERRELATIONS, THE RELATIONS WITHIN WHICH THESE INDIVIDUALS STAND."

This quotation seemed to encapsulate the idea of a collaborative quilt, the meaning of which stems not from the individual elements, but from the network of relationships among them. So I put out a call via my blog for collaborators in a secret project, and within twenty-four hours I had more than enough volunteers. I knew some of the people, and others were complete strangers (at that point). Many more knew each other or knew me through a friend; the network of relationships, and stories, compounded with each new member.

While I had a specific block design for the quilt—the vaguely figurative appliqué *i* as a stand-in for the individual—I wanted to impose as few controls as possible. Half the participants made blocks with solid backgrounds and prints for the *i*, and the other half used prints for the background and solids for the *i*. Color, style and technique were all left open to be a reflection of each individual in the group. What interested me were the ways in which they would all interrelate: the resonances and dissonances, the harmonies and contrasts. That's the thing about a healthy society; it admits and enfolds everyone, even the awkward ones, and in doing so, it finds its own greatest expression and reveals both the uniqueness and the commonality in every individual.

ON RANDOMNESS

Doing something truly random is nearly impossible, and improvisation rarely comes from out of the blue. Both are almost always based on a relatively simple system, whether one recognizes it or not. In fact, the best improvisations actually play off a rudimentary structure that allows for, and accommodates, a vast array of possibilities. In this quilt, I asked everybody to use fabric that they felt reflected their personality in some way. So for me, the fabric was somewhat random. But by alternating between solid and print backgrounds, the checkerboard structure facilitated the chaotic variations in fabric, technique and skill level.

The most intimidating part of doing an improvisation, or letting accidents happen, is generally the act of starting or, more specifically, the idea of starting from nothing. The hardest part of a new drawing is making that first mark because in so many ways it sets everything else in motion. Every drawing already has a complex system in place—from the size of the paper to the drawing medium—before that first mark even exists. By thinking about the structure you've set up, you, in fact, open yourself up to making that first mark and to the myriad unexpected results.

FINISHED SIZE

75½" × 75½" (191.8cm × 191.8cm)

MATERIALS LIST

- Each block uses two 6½" × 6½" (16.5cm × 16.5cm) squares of fabric, one solid and one print. For the quilt as shown, I used 121 block.

- Enough solid 6½" × 6½" (16.5cm × 16.5cm) squares to make a border for the quilt; the number needed will vary based on how many appliqué blocks are used to make up the quilt center. For this quilt, I used 48 squares for the border.

- 4 ²/₃ yards (4.3m) fabric for backing

- ½ yard (0.5m) fabric for binding

- Variegated yarn for tying

- The usual stuff you need to make a quilt (see page 14)

MAKING THE TOP

Using the template on page 116, cut out your appliqué pieces, cutting half of them from the solid squares and half from the print squares.

Center your appliqué pieces on the background square and attach using your preferred technique (see page 22 for the raw-edge appliqué technique). Remember to place solid appliqués on print squares and the print appliqués on solid squares.

Gather all of the blocks from everyone involved.

Lay out the appliquéd blocks alternating between solid and print backgrounds. Then lay out a border of solid blocks. You can also use a single color for a border or no border at all. This quilt is extremely flexible that way. Diagram 1.

Sew your blocks together, first into rows, and then sew those rows together. If using squares for the border, add those to the layout before sewing the rows together. If using a single color for the border, add those borders after the center unit is completed.

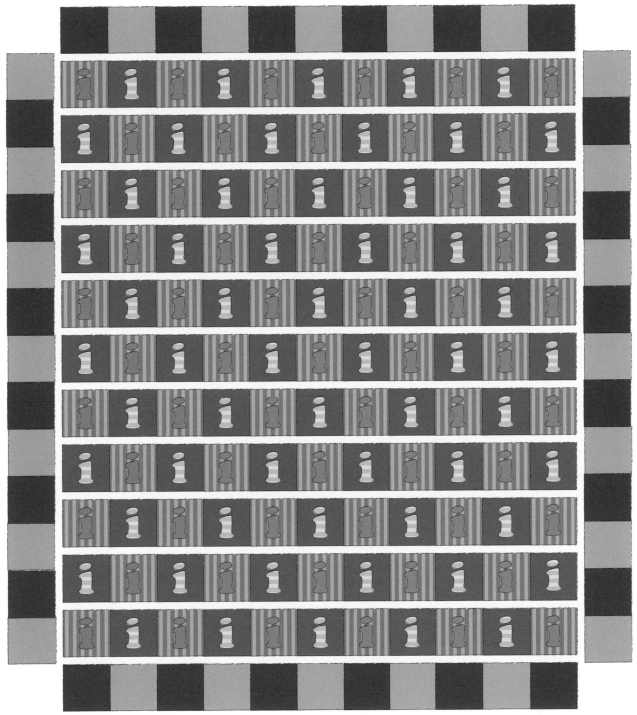

Diagram 1

FINISHING THE QUILT

After your top is completed, layer your backing right side down, your batting and the quilt top right side up. Baste the layers together. Of course you can quilt this however you like, but both conceptually and aesthetically, I think this quilt is perfect for being tied. I love the idea of tying the whole thing together both physically and metaphorically

Bind using your preferred method.

TYING A QUILT

There is something about tying a quilt that just feels right to me for a group project. The act of literally tying the whole thing together imparts a certain symbolic level to the quilt that satisfies the logical part of my brain. I also love the soft, supple quality of tied quilts; they just beg to be curled up under. Tied quilts speak to the essential practicality of quilts; while I love amazing quilting, tied quilts always remind me of the pragmatic need to hold those three layers together in a gesture that is simultaneously minimalist and extraordinarily traditional.

Generally, I tie a quilt of blocks at each seam intersection, unless the blocks are larger than 6" (15.2cm) square; in those cases, I figure out another arrangement.

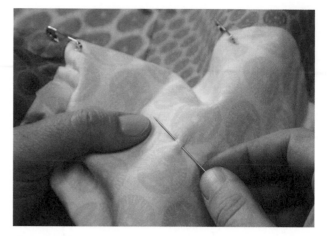

2 Thread a large embroidery needle with yarn or embroidery floss (I usually use a variegated pearl cotton). Push the needle through all three layers of the quilt and bring it back out approximately ⅛" (3mm) from where you inserted it.

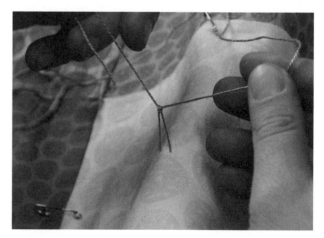

3 Pull the needle through, leaving a tail of yarn several inches (centimeters) long. Tie a double knot (I use a surgeon's knot, which is like a double square knot except you loop the tail through twice before tightening each knot rather than once). Pull the knot tight (but not so tight that the fabric puckers). Trim the ends of the yarn to about ½" (1.3cm).

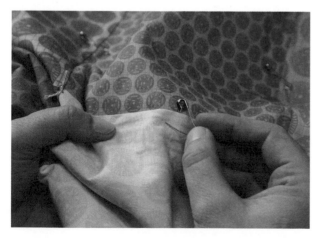

1 Baste the quilt with safety pins. I put pins close to the same spots where I'll add a tie.

WAYS TO MAKE THIS QUILT

For me, this quilt was all about illustrating the nature of the online community in which I participate. The fact that it took only twenty-four hours to have a full slate of volunteers for this quilt amazes me, and that so many of them didn't know me at all, at least not personally, showcases the generosity of that community. But that is just one way of engaging this quilt. I see this as a great quilt for responding to grief and joy, for celebration and loss. The essential premise of this quilt, of transforming individuals into a society of complex and resonant interrelations between fabric and people, speaks directly to the nature of the quilting bee and the symbolic and personal essence of quilts themselves.

Ani Hudson
Ann Marie Voigt
Anne Cullen
Ashley Yuckenberg
Audrie Bidwell
Barbara Stanbro
Becky Greene
Caey Gardonio-Foat
Caitlin McIntyre
Catherine Palmer
Cathleen Savage
Cathy Kizerian
Cecilia Young
Cheryl Ann Edholm
Chloe Read
Claudette Rocan
Colleen Yarnell
Collette Howie
Cori Ashley
Corinnea Martindale
Cristina Schweitzer
Cyndi Hoeller
Dan Rouse
Danielle Povey
Darci Barnhart
Debbie Grifka
DebbieKirkhope
Deedrie LaFollette
Denise Cargill
Douglas Carr
Earlene Springs
Ella Herrera
Erin Sampson
Flaun Cline
Freda Fields Alley
Ginerva Martin
Greta Minton
Hadley Jane Gordon
Hamish Dun
Heather Cap
Heide Mueller-Hatton
Helen Partridge
Hilary McFarlane
Holli Lofgren
Jane Davidson
Jenn Nevitt
Jennifer Bergman
Jeri Bonser
Jo Robertson
Joanna Kent
June Shen-Epstein
Karen Foster
Karen Ganske
Karen Marchetti
Karla Morriston
Kate Mehta
Kelley Gilbert
Kerryn Egel
Kim Tamok
Kimberly Lumapas
Kris Jarchow
Kristy Daum
Laurie Wisbrun
Linda Sandusky
Lisa Cockerham
Lisa Filion
Lisa Knell
Lisa Sipes
Lori Christensen
Louisa Budd
Louise Horler
Lucky Peterson
Lyn Mossett Regentin
Lynn Harris
Lynn Hurst
Lynne Johnson
Margaret Glendening
Marguerite Wiewel
Margy Merle
Marika Oullet
Marilyn Butler
Marsha Leith
Marti Dyer-Allison

For this label, I included the names of all the people who contributed blocks to the quilt.
This label, like those on most of my quilts, is pieced into the backing, so it's quilted as well.
See more on labels on page 24.

2 IDENTITY

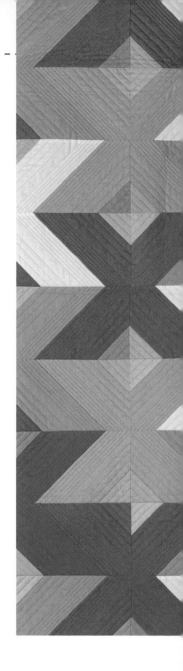

Quilts both shape and reflect us. The quilts we have been given and have lived with speak to us and tell us their stories; the quilts we make are manifestations of ourselves, or at least of our thoughts and passions. Either way, quilts are inextricably tied to their makers. Perhaps this is because of the investment of time and energy involved in making a quilt, or maybe it stems from the intimacy born of sleeping with a quilt night after night. Regardless of the reason, quilts seem to knit themselves into our lives and our identities.

While the relationship between a quilt and one's sense of identity is often oblique, there is also a robust tradition of quilts drawing directly upon issues of identity politics, responding to shifting understandings of one's self and one's relationship to the wider world. Samplers have long functioned as rites of passage, demonstrating a transition from novice to expert, evidence of a certain maturation. Story quilts tell us of lives and aspirations, hopes and losses.

Much of the visual vocabulary of quilting arises through the abstraction of life's details. What began as a figurative depiction transforms into a formal vocabulary open to endless variation. In those forms, in the often meticulous interweaving of shapes and colors, we see personal journeys, searches for private calm and celebrations of new possibilities.

The quilts in this section run a gamut of approaches to identity in quilts, from the search for a personal space to ways in which personal spaces interconnect to form a larger understanding of one's self. With each of these quilts, the material forms mirror the conceptual underpinning; the intended use of each quilt reflects the idea as much as the specific shapes that go into the composition. In many ways, these designs represent my most holistic approach to quilts as objects, moving beyond the bed or lap to investigate ways in which quilts can fit into our lives and make sense of ourselves.

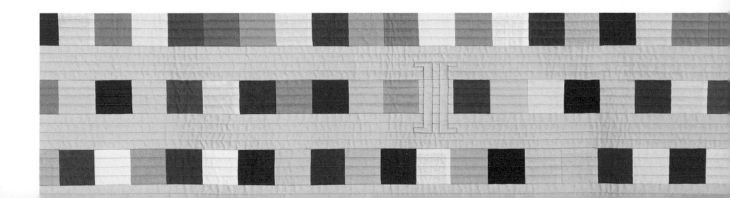

YOU ARE HERE

I've long been obsessed with You Are Here signs; they always seem to double as existential statements. More than just pinpointing a specific location within a mall or amusement park, they seem to be reminders that I do in fact exist, that for a moment at least I am not being pulled in a thousand directions by the continual chaos that is life. Right here and right now, I am simply here and nothing more.

Of course, that moment never lasts very long; there are always a multitude of *Here*s demanding my presence. I conceived this quilt as a meditation mat, one that singles out one possible Here from the abundance of possible Heres. Importantly, the Here that I emphasize does not occupy the central position; the quilt thus eschews the premise of being at the center of the universe and offers a metaphor for moving away from center stage for a moment of rest.

Whether this quilt is made as a meditation mat or a lap quilt, or expanded into a bed quilt by adding more blocks, I hope it serves as a double reminder: as a recognition of being—that you are indeed Here—and as a prompt to find a time and a space to pause, wherever that may be.

FINISHED SIZE

59" × 59" (149.9cm × 149.9cm)

MATERIALS LIST

- 1¼ yards (1.1m) Fabric 1

- 1¼ yards (1.1m) Fabric 2

- 1¼ yards (1.1m) Fabric 3

- 1¼ yards (1.1m) Fabric 4

- ⅓ yard (0.3m) Fabric 5

- 120 squares random scrap fabrics: 5¼" × 5¼" (13.3cm × 13.3cm)

- 4 yards (3.7m) fabric for backing

- ⅜ yard (0.3m) fabric for binding

- The usual stuff you need to make a quilt (see page 14)

NOTE: To help with your fabric selection, see Diagram 1 for fabric placement.

Diagram 2

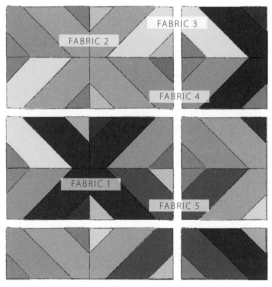

Diagram 1

CUTTING INSTRUCTIONS

From Fabric 1, cut 16 squares: 10⅞" × 10⅞" (27.6cm × 27.6cm)

From Fabric 2, cut 15 squares: 10⅞" × 10⅞" (27.6cm × 27.6cm)

From Fabric 3, cut 14 squares: 10⅞" × 10⅞" (27.6cm × 27.6cm)

From Fabric 4, cut 15 squares: 10⅞" × 10⅞" (27.6cm × 27.6cm)

From Fabric 5, cut 2 squares: 10⅞" × 10⅞" (27.6cm × 27.6cm)

MAKING THE BASIC BLOCK

Make a HST (half-square triangle) unit that will finish to 10" (25.4cm) using your preferred technique. I like to start with squares ⅞" (2.2cm) larger than the finished size, so in this case 10⅞" × 10⅞" (27.6m × 27.6cm). Stack two squares of different fabrics, right sides together, and draw a diagonal line from one corner to the opposite corner. Sew ¼" (6mm) on either side of that drawn line. Diagram 2.

Cut on the drawn line and press the seams toward the darker fabric. You will make two HST from each pair of 10⅞" (27.6cm) squares. Trim each HST to 10½" (26.7cm).

| Diagram 3 | Diagram 4 | Diagram 5 |

Make the following:

14 HST units with Fabric 1 and Fabric 3

16 HST units with Fabric 1 and Fabric 4

12 HST units with Fabric 2 and Fabric 3

14 HST units with Fabric 2 and Fabric 4

2 HST units with Fabric 1 and Fabric 5

2 HST units with Fabric 2 and Fabric 5

Once you have sewn the HST units, select two 5¼" (13.3cm) squares from the random color pile. Lay those squares on opposite corners of each HST unit that do not have the seam. Draw a line from corner to corner on the small squares, parallel to the sewn seam. Sew a seam along this line. Diagram 3.

Trim along the seams you just sewed to create a ¼" (6mm) seam allowance. Open the small triangles and press all seams toward the darker fabric. This unit should now measure 10½" (26.7cm) square. Diagram 4.

Trim 2" (5.1cm) from the top and bottom of the block you have just created. This is the basic block. This block should measure 10½" × 6½" (26.7cm × 16.5cm). Diagram 5. Make a total of 60 of these blocks from the HSTs listed above.

COMPOUND BLOCKS

Lately, I've been absolutely in love with half-square triangles (HSTs) and their various and sundry permutations. Most specifically, like in this quilt, I keep finding new ways to sew them together and then cut those blocks up in different ways to form complex shapes. While templates are great, there are so many possibilities out there when you just make a block and then cut it in some unexpected way.

Indeed, sometimes complexity is really complicated, but quite often it comes from a series of rather simple steps that build upon each other. In so many ways, this premise has been the guiding principle of Modernist design, just as it permeates the quilting tradition.

ASSEMBLING THE TOP

For this quilt, four blocks come together to form an *X*. But the trick is to get all the HST units in the right places (see Diagram 6) so the intertessellated *X*s all come together. While the finished design shows the quilt essentially as it will look, the function of the diagram below is to show just how the primary block elements (the legs of the *X*s) need to come together. The small triangles can be random, and it is perfectly fine if there are triangles of the same color in a diamond together.

FINISHING THE QUILT

After your top is completed, layer your backing right side down, your batting and the quilt top right side up. Baste the layers together, and then quilt as desired. For this quilt, Lisa developed a quilting approach that emphasized the diamonds in order to create a counter-rhythm to the prominent *X*s.

Bind using your preferred method.

Diagram 6

Credits: This top was pieced by Mary Kolb.

This quilt was pieced entirely using Essex Linens from Robert Kaufman.

MITOSIS

Making babies is fun—well, some of the time. The usual route doesn't work for everybody; at times, various degrees of medical assistance become necessary. Our first child happened in all the traditional ways—we actually locked ourselves out of our flat in our excitement at seeing a positive pregnancy test, which led to us "accidentally" buying a couple of stuffed monkeys—but our second child was conceived in a doctor's office.

Although the end result is the same—babies—I really wanted to design a quilt that spoke to the extraordinary fact that we were able to have our son, one that acknowledges and celebrates the transformation from clinical procedure to beloved individual. Mitosis is the process of cellular division; it's how babies (and just about everything else) grow. After a few rounds of intrauterine insemination (IUI), it becomes easy to lose sight of the bigger picture—baby—and become obsessed with the basic, scientific fact of needing two cells to get together. Hope and excitement give way to anxiety and doubt.

Mitosis (the quilt) begins with two squares, two colors. Those two colors carry over to the next set of four, all of which then carry over to the next set of eight, and so on. What starts as a simple mathematical progression evolves into a plenitude of color, the final set being composed of 128 different colors. The simple, blunt colors of the initial sets beget myriad modulated hues, while the sets themselves become subsumed into the totality of the design. The clinical, gray background only serves to set off the abundance of color, just as the doctor's office gives way to the extraordinary reality of a child.

FINISHED SIZE

62½" × 81" (158.8cm × 205.7cm)

MATERIALS LIST

- 1½ yards (1.4m) background fabric

- Fat quarter (45.7cm × 55.9cm) of 2 fabrics for Set 1

- Fat quarter (45.7cm × 55.9cm) of 2 fabrics for Set 2

- Fat quarter (45.7cm × 55.9cm) of 4 fabrics for Set 3

- Fat eighth (27.9cm × 45.7cm) of 8 fabrics for Set 4

- Fat eighth (27.9cm × 45.7cm) of 16 fabrics for Set 5

- Fat eighth (27.9cm × 45.7cm) or scraps of 32 fabrics for Set 6

- Fat eighth (27.9cm × 45.7cm) or scraps of 64 fabrics for Set 7

- 5 yards (5m) fabric for backing

- ½ yard (0.5m) fabric for binding

- The usual stuff you need to make a quilt (see page 14)

CUTTING INSTRUCTIONS

From background fabric:

Cut 4 strips: 40½" × 4½" (102.9cm × 11.4cm)

Cut 2 strips: 18½" × 4½" (47.0cm × 11.4cm)

Cut 12 strips: 40½" × 2½" (102.9cm × 6.4cm)

Fabrics:

Set 1: 2 fabrics each cut into 7 squares 2½" × 2½" (6.4cm × 6.4cm)

Set 2: 2 fabrics each cut into 6 squares 2½" × 2½" (6.4cm × 6.4cm)

Set 3: 4 fabrics each cut into 5 squares 2½" × 2½" (6.4cm × 6.4cm)

Set 4: 8 fabrics each cut into 4 squares 2½" × 2½" (6.4cm × 6.4cm)

Set 5: 16 fabrics each cut into 3 squares 2½" × 2½" (6.4cm × 6.4cm)

Set 6: 32 fabrics each cut into 2 squares 2½" × 2½" (6.4cm × 6.4cm)

Set 7: 64 colors each cut to 1 square 2½" × 2½" (6.4cm × 6.4cm)

PRINTS VS. SOLIDS

I had a really hard time deciding whether to do this quilt in prints or solids. There was a laundry list of reasons to go with either, but in the end, the idea of using 128 different Kona Solids, including all the subtle and in-between ones I never seem to use, just proved too tempting to resist. At the same time, building this quilt out of scraps to piece together a complicated whole seemed conceptually rich, with each print originally purchased for a different reason, part of some other life.

In so many ways, this quilt exemplifies my perpetual internal debate between solids and prints. I love the conceptual—and aesthetic—texture that prints bring, whereas an expansive array of solids allows me to play with complicated, hybrid tones that rarely find a home. For me, that choice is first a conceptual problem, a matching of material to idea, and only after that do the visual considerations come into play. Luckily there is rarely a wrong answer, just different ways to direct the conversation.

PIECING THE TOP

Separate all of your 2½" (6.4cm) squares into their proper group. Group 1 has the two colors from Set 1. Group 2 has one of each from Sets 1 and 2. Group 3 has one of each from Sets 1, 2 and 3, and so on until Group 7, which has one from all seven sets. The total number of squares in each group should be:

Group 1: 2 squares

Group 2: 4 squares

Group 3: 8 squares

Group 4: 16 squares

Group 5: 32 squares

Group 6: 64 squares

Group 7: 128 squares

Cut one 40½" × 2½" (102.9cm × 6.4cm) background strip into 2½" × 2½" (6.4cm × 6.4cm) squares. You will need 6 of these gray squares.

Sew together all of your rows. Specific placement of squares within the groups is random as long as the groups are properly separated by background squares.

Sew together your completed rows of squares, separating each with a 40½" × 2½" (102.9cm × 6.4cm) background sashing strip. Diagram 1.

Diagram 1

Sew one 40½" × 4½" (102.9cm × 11.4cm) border strip to the top of the quilt top and one to the bottom.

Sew together your remaining background pieces to make the two long side border strips; these should end up 58½" × 4½" (148.6cm × 11.4cm). Attach these borders to the sides of the center, and the top is finished. Diagram 2.

FINISHING THE QUILT

After your top is completed, layer your backing right side down, your batting and the quilt top right side up. Baste the layers together, and then quilt as desired. For this quilt, Lisa and I decided on simple, straight lines to reinforce the simplicity of the design structure and to allow the brackets for each cellular grouping of color squares to stand out.

Bind using your preferred method.

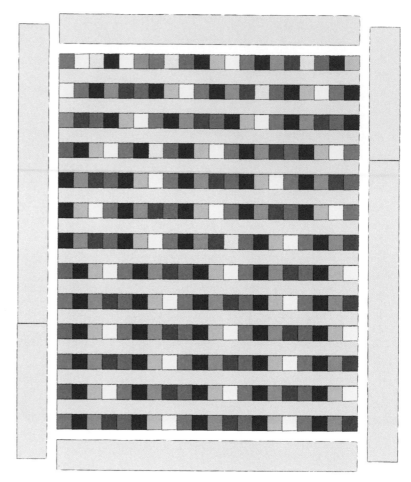

Diagram 2

QUILTING (AGAIN)

Quilting doesn't have to be fancy to be important; sometimes the simplest gesture can truly bring a quilt—and the idea behind it—to life. While the horizontal straight lines reinforce the cool minimalism of the design, the addition of the subtly color-coded brackets—they progress through all seven colors of the rainbow—clarifies the mathematic progression behind the design of the quilt. So many times the complicated answer is the right way to go, but every once in a while, a simpler (and hopefully smarter) answer really is better.

Credit: This quilt was pieced entirely with Kona Solids from Robert Kaufman.

REUNION

Long-distance relationships have been a constant part of my life. My parents lived in separate towns for as long as I can remember; my wife and I spent nine of our first fifteen years together in different cities, or even countries. This is growing more and more common: when children leave home, they really move away, and multiple generations of a single family living in the same town is becoming the exception rather than the rule.

Long-distance relationships themselves are peculiar things; in many ways, they are similar to quantum theory—they necessitate a particular and inextricable connection at a distance. Even as I lived a thousand miles from my wife, she was always profoundly present. Her absence always occupied space in my mind and in my home; I even set up an office in my apartment for her that was purely hers, even though she was only there a few weeks a year. The potential of her being there made her seem somehow less distant; her absence became a merely provisional thing, a time between visits.

Reunion is made up of four quilts, though you can make it with more or fewer; each quilt has buttons and loops sewn into the binding so the quilts can be joined together to form a larger, family-sized quilt. On one level, the loops and buttons sewn into the binding allow the individual quilts—one for each member of a family or group—to form that larger whole, just as a family is made up of individuals. At the same time, those loops and buttons serve as a continual reminder of that larger whole when the individual quilts are used separately, becoming a permanent residue of that fundamental connection. For this quilt, or set of quilts, the specific pattern of each quilt is far less important than the superstructure that they create.

I have always envisioned these quilts as a picnic set: each quilt large enough for a picnic for one—a pastry and a cup of coffee with a book under the shade of a tree—and when they all come together, large enough for an entire family. Of course, they're adaptable enough to allow any number of the quilts to be together for a visit or to allow for a new addition. *Reunion* is essentially a metaphor for the new, changing family structures that are emerging, even as it evokes a certain bucolic idealism.

FINISHED SIZE

Each quilt is 49" × 49" (124.5cm × 124.5cm); four quilts combined are 99" × 99" (251.5cm × 251.5cm)

MATERIALS LIST FOR EACH QUILT

- 11 fat quarters (45.7cm × 55.9cm) print fabric
- 3 fat quarters (45.7cm × 55.9cm) solid fabric
- 2¼ yard (2.1m) fabric for backing
- ⅓ yard (0.3m) fabric for binding
- 4 yards (3.7m) ⅛" (3mm) wide satin ribbon
- 8 buttons for each quilt
- Large-eyed embroidery needle
- The usual stuff you need to make a quilt (see page 14)

CUTTING

For each quilt: 169 squares cut to 4½" × 4½" (11.4cm × 11.4cm) squares. I used 11 different prints and 3 different solids for each quilt as follows:

Quilt 1: 152 print squares, 17 solid squares

Quilt 2: 142 print squares, 27 solid squares

Quilt 3: 143 print squares, 26 solid squares

Quilt 4: 150 print squares, 19 solid squares

PIECING THE TOPS

Piece your squares into rows according to Diagrams 1–4, and then piece those rows together to complete your tops.

ON INSPIRATION

So often we expect inspiration to be big and revelatory, but in my experience, that rarely happens. Those giant, brilliant ideas are generally the result of days, weeks and months of labor. Luckily, there are millions of bits of inspiration in our lives, the details and nuances that make life wonderful and meaningful. Those bits are rarely monumental, but that doesn't mean they aren't significant.

The design of each of the *Reunion* quilts was inspired by the cartoon *Battle of the Planets* that aired in the U.S. in the late 1970s; both my wife and I loved that cartoon when we were kids. One of my most vivid memories of the show was that each of the main characters wore a shirt with a number on it; I've loved big, graphic numbers ever since. In making these quilts, I let my daughter choose who got which number, each choice important to her for private—and a little bit inscrutable—reasons. Sometimes quilts speak to big ideas; other times they hold secret and hidden meanings. And sometimes, in the best of cases, they do both.

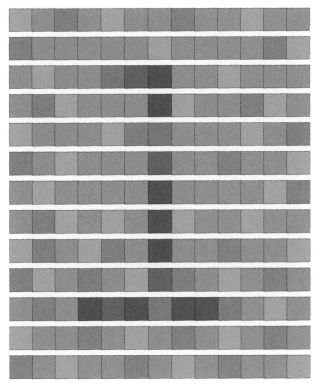

Diagram 1

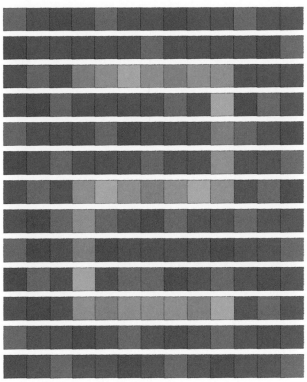

Diagram 2

Diagram 3

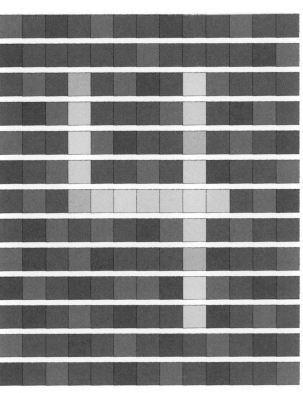

Diagram 4

FINISHING THE QUILTS

After your top is completed, layer your backing right side down, your batting and the quilt top right side up. Baste the layers together, and then quilt as desired. For these quilts, Lisa and I went with a quilting approach that would subtly counter the simple grid of each quilt and become a larger pattern when the quilts came together.

ATTACHING THE RIBBON LOOPS AND BUTTONS

Using your sewing machine, attach the binding to the front of each quilt. Then follow the steps below.

On these quilts, I placed the buttons and loops on the third seam from each corner.

To connect the quilts, arrange the quilts so the loops and buttons align, then slip the buttons on both quilts through the loops on the adjacent quilt.

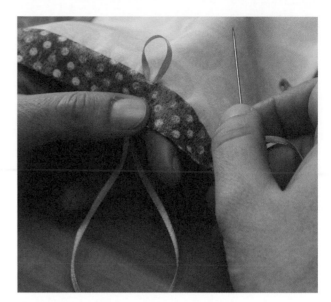

2 Push the needle back through to the underside, leaving a 1" (2.5cm) loop of ribbon on the top of the quilt.

3 To help keep your loop sizes consistent, you can put a small spool of thread through the loop and pull it tight.

1 Thread the satin ribbon through the large-eyed needle. Pull your ribbon through to the top of the quilt, starting from the underside of the binding, about ⅛" (3mm) from the edge of the quilt.

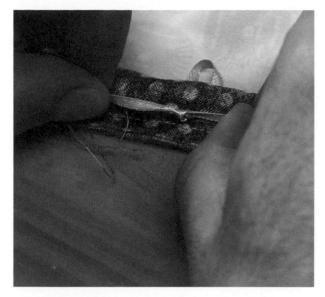

4 Trim the ribbon and tie a triple square knot in the tail ends.

5 Holding the loop down toward the edge of the quilt, sew a button on top of each loop with a needle and thread. Be sure to secure the button very, very well.

Once all of the loops and buttons are attached, hand stitch your binding to the back of the quilt. Repeat for all the quilts in your group.

ON WORKING WITH SINGLE COLLECTIONS

There are times when a quilt starts with me staring at my stash and pulling fabrics out; I first build a massive pile of possibilities and then winnow it down (or not). Other times, a single fabric collection truly speaks to the ideas behind a quilt. I look at working with a collection as a challenge, as an opportunity to interpret that collection and respond to the designer's intent, to pay my respects to that designer. Perhaps that is the fabric designer in me wanting to pair my voice as a quilter with that of the fabric designer in a sort of duet.

In the *Reunion* suite, I specifically selected each collection as a means to represent how I perceive the subjects of each quilt: my wife, my daughter, my son and myself. When those different fabric voices come together, they form a larger conversation, one that I hope, in some small way, reflects the spirit of my family. Every collection is more than an aesthetic, a compilation of designs; it embodies an ethos, a position, a character.

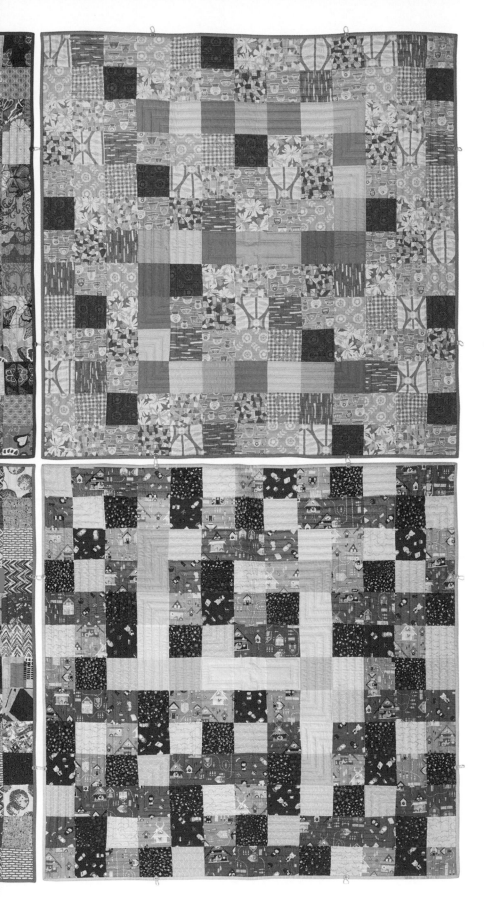

Credits: These quilts were pieced using
the following fabric collections:

Quilt 1:
Cocoon by Valori Wells
for FreeSpirit Fabric

Quilt 2:
La Dee Da by Erin McMorris
for FreeSpirit Fabric

Quilt 3:
Center City by Jay McCarroll
for FreeSpirit Fabric

Quilt 4:
Storybook Lane by Kelly Lee-Creel

3 SOCIAL COMMENTARY

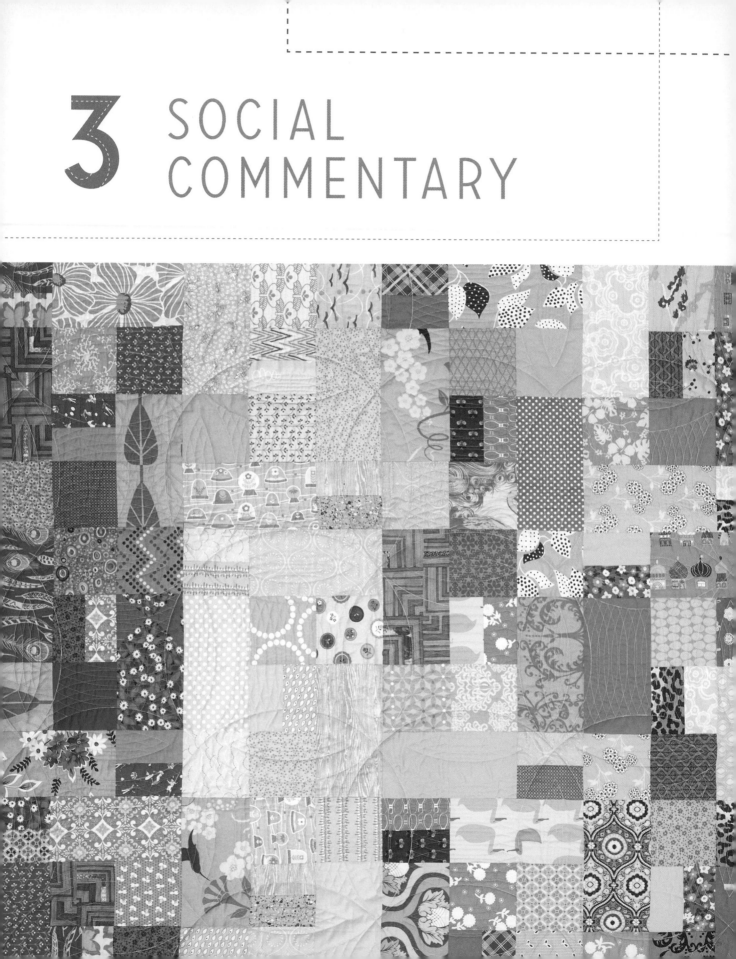

The idea of stitching diverse ideas together has long seemed an apt metaphor for intertwining complicated concepts and commentaries, a means not only for expression but also for analysis and engagement. Kara Walker, Faith Ringgold and the AIDS quilt inspired me, showing me the extraordinary potential of wedding the quilting heritage to political and social activism, and further led me to see how vital such practices have always been to quilting.

In recent decades, social and political commentary has largely been the purview of the Art Quilt community, as its technical and material freedom lends itself to a wider range of expression and offers a deeper toolbox to speak to issues and concerns. As such, quilters drawn to activism through their quilts have often been drawn away from the spaces and practices of traditional/practical quilts.

For me, there is something unique about the marriage of practical, usable quilts with the examination of serious social and political issues. There is something profound and powerful about wrapping oneself up in a message, living and sleeping with it. The idea, the commentary, becomes a part of one's life, a reflection and reminder of how a person wishes to live. Rather than turn to impractical materials and methods, each quilt here seeks to use the visual and technical vocabulary of practical quilts in order to create pieces that address serious social issues to bring commentary to the spaces of our everyday lives.

The projects in this section represent just a few of the issues I hope to address with my quilts; they are signposts toward a discussion of how we see practical quilts, examinations of an expanding vocabulary as well as a repatriation of an activist thread. They are sites for making meaning as well as forms, for speaking out, for being heard. They commemorate and memorialize; they insist and plead. These quilts speak to the tragic and the mundane, the extraordinary and the abhorrent. Most importantly, these quilts speak.

IN DEFENSE OF HANDMADE

like words. Ask anyone who's met me, and they'll agree. Some might roll their eyes at how much I seem to like words. Language and the details of how we use it really matter to me; what we say and how we say it reflect what is important to us as individuals and as a society. That is why I experienced a minor epiphany when I first encountered a quilt that was factory-made in China from a "handcrafted pattern."

The word "handmade" has been stretched to near the breaking point. What was once a necessity and then an ethos is now a style. In so many cases, what matters is not the labor and love that goes into creating something but the decorative statement that comes with something looking handmade. The world is replete with carefully dented woodwork, prefaded furnishings and mass-produced reproductions of originally handcrafted creations. The handmade look has become a style.

In Defense of Handmade turns this commodification of the handmade around on itself. Using the UPC symbol of a mass-produced quilt as a starting point, this quilt takes the point of sale as a point of inspiration. The ubiquitous bar code becomes a place for color and play, for injecting individuality and personality in lieu of the homogeneity of the factory-made. The rigid perfection of the bar code stripes gives way to the subtle variation of the handicraft, reflecting the texture of a lived life rather than a simple purchase.

In Defense of Handmade not only glories in the individuality of handmade things, it also honors the labor of making, the time spent with the materials themselves. This quilt is about the giving of oneself that is such a part of a quilter's life. While the physical object of a quilt may be packaged up and sold, the devotion embedded within handmade quilts can never be adequately quantified.

FINISHED SIZE

88½" × 88½" (224.8cm × 224.8cm)

MATERIALS LIST

- ¼ yard (0.2m) each of 16 print fabrics

- 12 squares of print fabrics: 8" × 8" (20.3cm × 20.3cm) for appliquéd numbers

- 7 yards (6.4m) white (or other solid)

- 7½ yards (6.9m) fabric for backing

- ⅝ yard (0.6m) fabric for binding

- The usual stuff you need to make a quilt (see page 14)

CUTTING INSTRUCTIONS

Note: WOF = width of fabric

From each of the 16 prints:

    Cut 2 strips: 4½" × WOF (11.4cm × WOF)

From white (background solid):

    Cut 1 strip: 64½" × WOF (163.8cm × WOF) for bar code strips

    Cut 2 A strips: 45" × 11" (114.3cm × 27.9cm)

    Cut 2 B strips: 45" × 10" (114.3cm × 25.4cm)

    Cut 2 C strips: 60" × 16" (152.4cm × 40.6cm)

    Cut 2 D strips: 22" × 9" (55.9cm × 22.9cm)

    Cut 2 E strips: 16" × 9" (40.6cm × 22.9cm)

    Cut 2 F pieces: 6½" × 4½" (16.5cm × 11.4cm)

    Cut 1 G piece: 2½" × 4½" (6.4cm × 11.4cm)

THINGS ARE COMPLICATED

What is handmade? This may seem like a simple question, but the more I think about it, the more complicated it gets. I use a sewing machine; I design on a computer; there are endless technological aids to my practice. For me, the nature of handmade stems from the maker's relationship to the practice of making, which can run an extraordinary gamut of personal, economic and social circumstances. What draws me to the community of makers is the notion that the practice itself matters, that there is indeed a real difference between the style and substance of things.

PIECING THE STRIPS

Split your 4½" × WOF (11.4cm × WOF) print strips into two groups of 16 strips each, distributing the colors equally.

With right sides together, piece the strips along the long edges, creating two large panels, each measuring 64½" × WOF (163.8cm × WOF). Label one panel #1 and the other panel #2. Press all the seams in the same direction.

Beginning with panel #1, cut strips perpendicular to the already sewn seams. The chart below provides you with the cut width for each strip and that strip's position in the finished quilt for panel #1, panel #2 and the white background fabric.

For example, on panel #1, the first cut will be 1⅛" × 64½" (2.9cm × 163.8cm). The second cut will be 2¼" × 64½" (5.7cm × 163.8cm), etc. Repeat the same procedure for panel #2, with the first cut being 1⅛" × 64½" (2.9cm × 163.8cm). As you cut, number each strip according to the chart.

From the solid 64½" × WOF (163.8cm × WOF) background piece, cut strips using the same chart. Number these strips, too.

STRIP CUTTING AND NUMBERING CHART

PANEL #1

STRIP POSITION	STRIP WIDTH
1	1⅛" (2.9cm)
5	2¼" (5.7cm)
9	2⅞" (7.3cm)
13	2⅞" (7.3cm)
17	1¾" (4.4cm)
21	1¾" (4.4cm)
25	2⅞" (7.3cm)
29	1⅛" (2.9cm)
33	1¼" (3.2cm)
37	1¾" (4.4cm)
41	1¾" (4.4cm)
45	1¾" (4.4cm)
49	1⅛" (2.9cm)
53	1¾" (4.4cm)
57	1⅛" (2.9cm)

PANEL #2

STRIP POSITION	STRIP WIDTH
3	1⅛" (2.9cm)
7	1¾" (4.4cm)
11	1⅛" (2.9cm)
15	1⅛" (2.9cm)
19	1⅛" (2.9cm)
23	1⅛" (2.9cm)
27	1⅛" (2.9cm)
31	1¼" (3.2cm)
35	2¼" (5.7cm)
39	1¾" (4.4cm)
43	1¾" (4.4cm)
47	1¾" (4.4cm)
51	1⅛" (2.9cm)
55	1¾" (4.4cm)
59	1⅛" (2.9cm)

BACKGROUND FABRIC

STRIP POSITION	STRIP WIDTH	STRIP POSITION	STRIP WIDTH
2	1" (2.5cm)	32	1" (2.5cm)
4	1⅛" (2.9cm)	34	1⅞" (4.8cm)
6	1⅛" (2.9cm)	36	1" (2.5cm)
8	1" (2.5cm)	38	1⅛" (2.9cm)
10	1⅛" (2.9cm)	40	1⅝" (4.1cm)
12	1" (2.5cm)	42	1" (2.5cm)
14	1⅛" (2.9cm)	44	1¾" (4.4cm)
16	2⅜" (6.0cm)	46	1" (2.5cm)
18	1⅛" (2.9cm)	48	1⅝" (4.1cm)
20	2⅛" (5.4cm)	50	1" (2.5cm)
22	1⅛" (2.9cm)	52	2¾" (7.0cm)
24	1⅛" (2.9cm)	54	1⅝" (4.1cm)
26	1⅛" (2.9cm)	56	1" (2.5cm)
28	1" (2.5cm)	58	1⅛" (2.9cm)
30	1⅛" (2.9cm)		

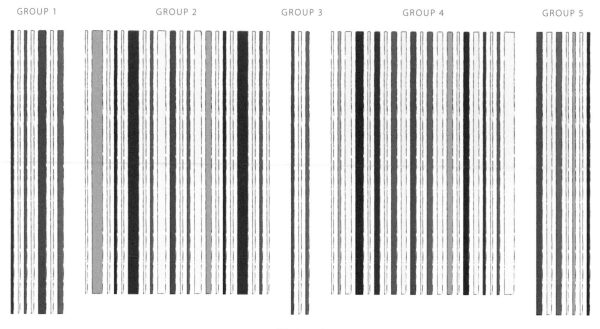

Diagram 1

Lay out the strips in numerical order from left to right. Divide the strips into five groups as follows:

Group 1: strips 1–7

Group 2: strips 8–28

Group 3: strips 29–31

Group 4: strips 32–52

Group 5: strips 53–59

Pin the strips liberally so they don't stretch and curve as you sew the long seams. (I pin every two seams.)

Trim Group 2 and Group 4 to 59½" (151.1cm) long to accommodate the appliqué numbers in the UPC symbol. Be sure to trim from the bottom of the group so the order of the prints in the strips remains consistent when you piece everything together. Diagram 1.

APPLIQUÉING THE NUMBERS

Using the number templates on pages 118–123 and your preferred appliqué method, appliqué the numbers as follows. All numbers should be 1" (2.5cm) from the bottom of the fabric. The outer numbers should be approximately 3" (7.6cm) from the edge of the fabric.

PINS, PINS, PINS

When piecing long, skinny strips, especially ones that have been strip-pieced, there is a big tendency for one piece of fabric to stretch a bit more than the other, which will turn straight lines into subtle (or not so subtle) curves. This is where pins are your best friend, even if you generally don't use or need them. Pin the ends of your strips together, evenly distribute the fabric in between and pin periodically. Your seams will end up nice and straight, and your top will come out happy and flat.

Onto one background strip D, appliqué the numbers 33003.

Onto the second background strip D, appliqué the numbers 52226.

Onto one background strip E, appliqué the number 7 to the far right side.

Onto the second background strip E, appliqué the number 1 to the far left side.

PIECING THE TOP

Piece together the two background A strips at one short end. Piece together the two background B strips at the short end.

Sew background strip E with the number 7 appliqué to the bottom of one background strip C. Sew background strip E with the number 1 appliqué to the bottom of the second background strip C.

Sew one background piece F to the bottom of strip Group 1. Sew the second background piece F to the bottom of strip Group 5.

Sew background strip D with the 33003 appliqué to the bottom of strip Group 2. Sew the remaining background strip D with the 52226 appliqué to the bottom of strip Group 4.

Sew background piece G to the bottom of strip Group 3.

Sew the number 7 appliqué strip to the Group 1 strip. Sew the Group 2 strip to the Group 1 strip. Sew the Group 3 strip to the Group 2 strip. Sew the Group 4 strip to the Group 3 strip. Sew the Group 5 strip to the Group 4 strip. Sew the number 1 appliqué strip to the Group 5 strip. Press each seam before sewing on the next strip.

Sew the background A strips to the top of the quilt. Sew the background B strips to the bottom of the quilt top.

Your top should measure 88½" (224.8cm) square.

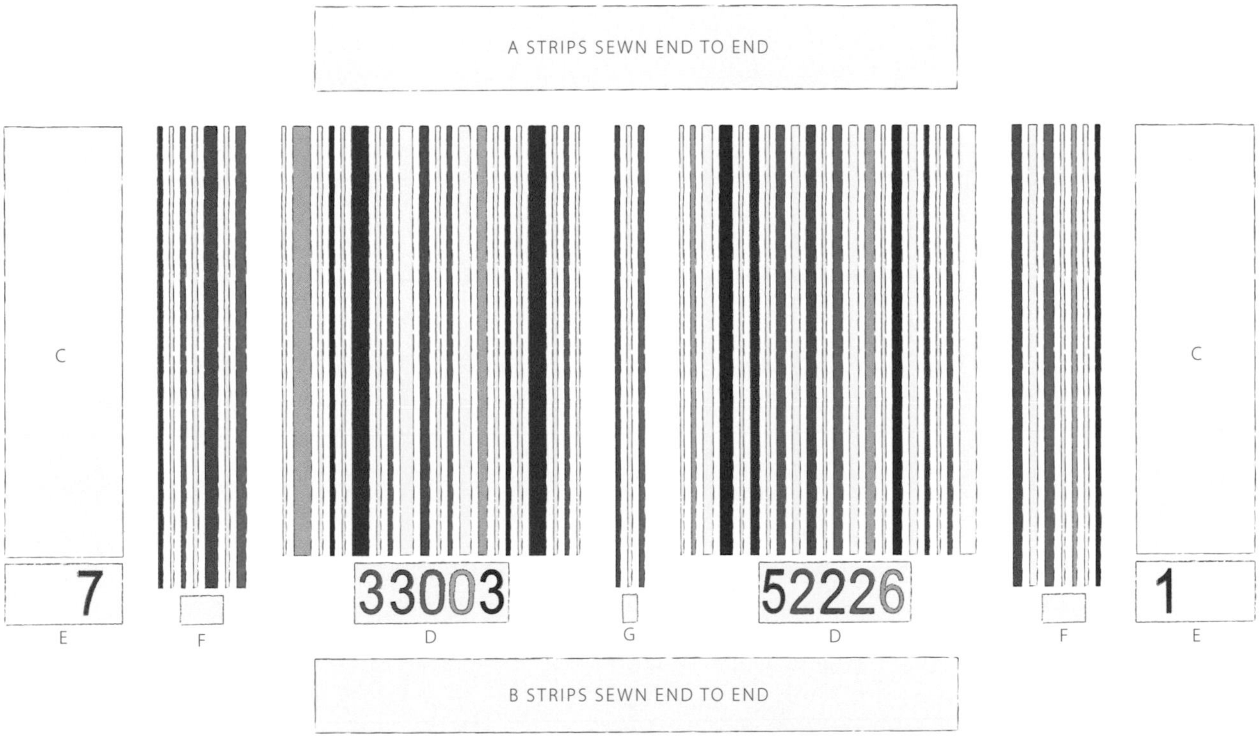

A STRIPS SEWN END TO END

7 · E
F
33003 · D
G
52226 · D
F
1 · E

B STRIPS SEWN END TO END

FINISHING THE QUILT

After your top is completed, layer your backing right side down, your batting and the quilt top right side up. Baste the layers together, and then quilt as desired. Bind using your preferred method.

For this quilt, Lisa went all the way. It speaks both to the craft and skill of quilting, while still putting the design and concept of the quilt first.

The first step was to trapunto the quilt title into the quilt; adding in the quilt title allowed us to make explicit the cultural critique that inspired this quilt. For trapunto, you first layer the top and batting and carefully quilt specific areas and designs—in this case the letters. You then cut away the excess batting from around those shapes; this adds an extra layer of batting, and thus loft, to the selected areas of the quilt. From there, the typical quilting process resumes, with the top, batting and backing sandwiched together. We decided to go with trapunto for this quilt both as a nod to traditional quilting practices within a very untraditional design, and as a means of distancing the quilt from the quick and easy techniques used for the mass-produced quilt the bar code was based upon.

With the second stage of quilting, Lisa again went above and beyond, utilizing three subtly different thread colors to execute the overall quilting pattern. Furthermore, in never quilting over the prints, she produced three different visual layers on the surface of the quilt: the trapunto, the prints and the densely quilted white spaces. Doing so required an enormous amount of tying off of thread ends between all the columns of the bar code itself. As a sly gesture, she quilted this at 20 stitches per inch (2.5cm) as a rebuke to the large and flimsy stitches used in mass-produced quilts.

In the end, every step in the making of this quilt was considered in response to the idea of and practices involved in mass-producing quilts. The bar code strips are patchwork rather than single pieces of fabric; the quilting is intricate and laborious while remaining surprisingly subtle. At every stage, the goal was to highlight those small decisions that come from the act of making, to carefully wed the conceptual and the material, to challenge the disposability that the bar code symbolizes.

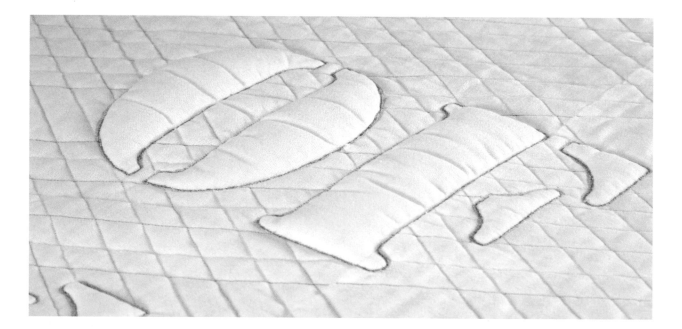

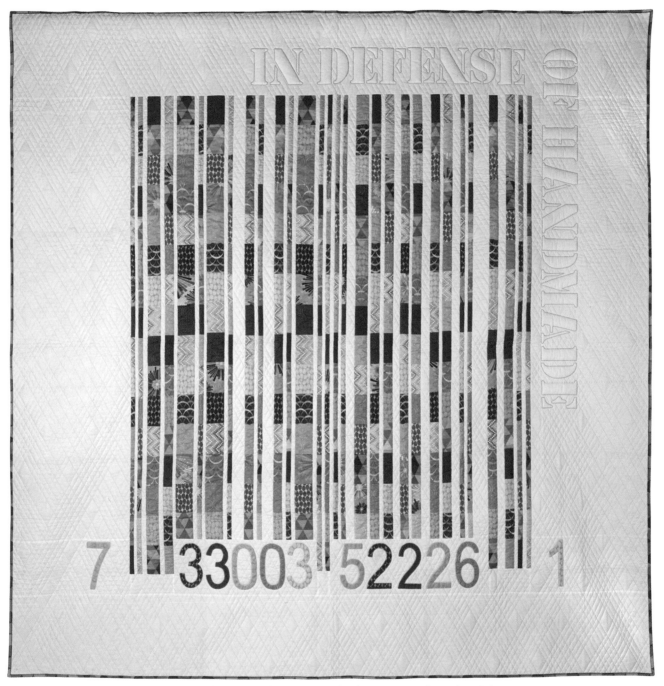

Credit: This quilt was pieced using Frippery by Thomas Knauer for Andover Fabrics.

PALIMPSEST (PRIDE FLAG)

knew that I wanted to do a quilt about same-sex marriage for this book, but I struggled to find an appropriate form, one that simultaneously spoke to the personal and political aspects of the issue. In working through my ideas, I kept returning to the iconic images of the Pride Flag and the Double Wedding Ring quilt. Each of these forms has come to stand as a sort of shorthand for a wealth of social and cultural beliefs: the Pride Flag stands as a symbol of gay rights, and the Double Wedding Ring speaks to the long-standing tradition of marriage. But any attempt to fit the one form into the other seemed to subordinate one of the elements instead of expressing a fundamental harmony, until I struck upon the idea of the palimpsest.

At its core, a palimpsest is a document in which one text is written over another; the one text may efface the other to a greater or lesser degree, but ultimately, the two texts reside in the same space, forming a hybrid document or co-writing. Even as the palimpsest facilitates the compression of ideas into a common dialogue, it also allows an extraordinary liberation of forms. Unlike marginalia, in which one text wraps around and responds to another, in a palimpsest, the two texts are written independently, each one manifesting its own formal and conceptual space. In translating the idea of the palimpsest into a quilt, it can mean that the quilting is completely liberated from the piecing; each follows its own logic and produces its own forms. The ultimate expression of the quilt emerges in the interplay of the two distinct writings: the piecing and the quilting.

In *Palimpsest (Pride Flag)*, because gay pride and marriage share the same space, one form is seen through the other, the ideas and forms become entangled, inextricably bound together. Fitting the colors of the Pride Flag into the forms of the Double Wedding Ring would lend a certain priority to the forms of that traditional wedding quilt, placing one concept within the logic of another. Instead, the writing of the Double Wedding Ring into the same space as the Pride Flag subverts the idea of an ordinary logic, the notion that one element must conform or accede to another. In allowing both piecing and quilting to find their own best expression, the palimpsest as a quilt speaks to the complexities of both experience and form.

WHY POLITICS

All politics are personal in one way or another; our views generally reflect our most personal beliefs and stem from the richest stories of our lives. I do not make quilts that deal with social and political issues solely to make a statement, but because the issues involved are intimately connected to my life. This first Palimpsest quilt comes from and is for a family member—actually two family members, regardless of the current laws of the land. This quilt is a gesture, however small, in recognizing their relationship as no less significant, no less valid than my marriage. In my mind, that is the essence of quilts; they are gestures, expressions of care and concern, compassion and thought. It is when the public and the personal components of quilts are seamlessly integrated that I find quilts the most compelling; it is then that they reveal a profound, enduring value. That ideal is what I strive toward with every quilt and, hopefully, sometimes achieve.

FINISHED SIZE

62½" × 69½" (158.8cm × 176.5cm)

MATERIALS LIST

- A minimum of 11 different prints or solids for each color stripe. This quilt works best if you just pull from your fabric stash. If you don't have a big stash or a large array of colors, it can also be done with fat quarters (45.7cm × 55.9cm), fat eighths (27.9cm × 45.7cm) or ⅛ yard (0.1m) cuts.

- 4 yards (3.7m) fabric for backing

- ½ yard (0.5m) fabric for binding

- The usual stuff you need to make a quilt (see page 14)

CUTTING INSTRUCTIONS

For each color stripe you will need to cut the following:

    12 pieces: 8½" × 4½" (21.6cm × 11.4cm)

    16 squares: 4½" × 4½" (11.4cm × 11.4cm)

    16 pieces: 2½" × 4½" (6.4cm × 11.4cm)

Make sure you have at least one of each print in each size.

PIECING THE BLOCKS

Sew two of your 2½" × 4½" (6.4cm × 11.4cm) pieces together to make a 4½" × 4½" (11.4cm × 11.4cm) square. Make two of these units.

First sew one of the new units to a 4½" × 4½" (11.4cm × 11.4cm) square and then sew that unit to one of your 8½" × 4½" (21.6cm × 11.4cm) pieces to form Group A. Diagram 1.

Next sew the other pieced unit to one of your 8½" × 4½" (21.6cm × 11.4cm) pieces to form Group B.

Piece together two 4½" × 4½" (11.4cm × 11.4cm) squares to form Group C.

Piece together one 4½" × 4½" (11.4cm × 11.4cm) square and one 8½" × 4½" (21.6cm × 11.4cm) piece to form Group D.

Sew Group C to Group A. Sew Group D to the bottom of Group C/A. Sew Group B to the right side of Group C/A/D.

Make four of these blocks for each row, making sure to mix the fabrics.

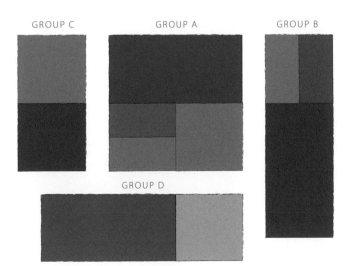

GROUP C   GROUP A   GROUP B

GROUP D

Diagram 1

PIECING THE ROWS

The important things about piecing the rows is that the orientation of the block is rotated 180° for alternating blocks.

Start rows 1, 3 and 5 with Group A oriented at the bottom of the block. For the next block in these rows, rotate the block 180° so Group A is at the top. Repeat across these rows.

Start rows 2, 4 and 6 with Group A at the top of the block. For the next block in these rows, rotate the block 180° so Group A is at the top. Repeat across these rows.

After your rows are pieced, sew them together making sure they are in the correct color order: red, orange, yellow, green, blue and then purple, going from the top to the bottom of the quilt.

FINISHING THE QUILT

After your top is completed, layer your backing right side down, your batting and the quilt top right side up. Baste the layers together, and then quilt as desired. While the quilting decisions are evident for this one, the choice to keep the quilting light and gentle is all about letting this quilt be an everyday quilt, rather than a precious object, which in itself serves as a metaphor.

Bind using your preferred method.

EXCESS

Every year approximately 1,600 women and men are killed in acts of domestic violence in the United States, victimized by their partners and spouses. Far too often the legal system, driven by an odd mixture of social conventions and political realities, is left powerless to prevent these deaths. We seem squeamish about interfering in domestic situations, even as we lament each loss. We appear to be unable to see the forest for the trees, as though we fear admitting the prevalence of domestic abuse within our own society.

Excess is a memorial to this overwhelming reality, a visualization of the forest of loss. Each of the 1,600 squares in the quilt represents a death, with each red or orange stripe a woman killed, and each blue or green one a man. The quilt utilizes the stark repetition of forms to illustrate the painful monotony of these deaths, the seemingly endless progression of loss and suffering, even as the variety of prints lends individuality to each block. The result is a memorial that hangs over 13' (4.0m) long so that it pools on the floor, too monumental to fit on most walls. The individual squares accumulate to form something larger than a wall can bear, producing a figurative call to action in response to this unbearable violence.

The basis of any memorial is that in the recognition of the loss and the admission of our horror, we might find hope for something better, a path toward a solution or at least the impetus to begin that journey. Memorials give voice to our collective sorrow and serve as a locus for coming together. I see *Excess* as an opportunity for people and communities to come together, to resist the silence that too often pervades domestic abuse.

As a quilt, *Excess* taps into the profound heritage of quilts as memorials, as documents that mark a moment in history, objects that compel us to deal with our individual and collective pasts. Rather than comfort or celebrate, though, *Excess* confronts viewers with its material excess, which is the essence of the memorial itself.

ON MODERN

In a lot of cases, modern quilting has been identified with large-scale piecing and bright bold colors, but I am always nervous about defining things through just a few of their common attributes. For me, modern quilting is more about a perspective, a way of approaching the practice of quilting, the way one incorporates it within a world view. The shapes, colors and scales are all secondary for me, tools of the trade rather than defining features. As such, small work can be and is a rich part of the modern quilting vocabulary. The very idea of obsessive, repetitive acts launched an entire Modernist movement—Process Art. What matters is fitting the techniques and styles to the concept, wherever that may take us.

FINISHED SIZE

40½" × 160½" (102.9cm × 407.7cm)

MATERIALS LIST

- 5½ yards (5.0m) white or another light, neutral solid
- A massive pile of orange and red scraps
- A smaller pile of blue and green scraps
- 5 yards (4.6m) fabric for backing
- ⅝ yard (0.6m) fabric for binding
- Variegated yarn for tying
- The usual stuff you need to make a quilt (see page 14)

NOTE: You can also use a bunch of jelly rolls or fat eighths (27.9cm × 45.7cm), but this quilt just gets better when it has more diversity.

CUTTING

From white or neutral solid, cut 3,200 squares: 1½" × 1½"(3.8cm × 3.8cm)

From orange and red scraps, cut 1,280 squares: 2½" × 2½" (6.4cm × 6.4cm)

From blue and green scraps, cut 320 squares: 2½" × 2½" (6.4cm × 6.4cm)

PIECING THE UNITS

With one of your 2½" (6.4cm) squares right side up, place one 1½" (3.8cm) neutral square in the top left corner and one in the bottom right corner. Sew each small square as shown in Diagram 1.

Trim the seam allowances to ¼" (6mm). Press the neutral pieces back as in Diagram 2.

Repeat with all 1,600 2½" (6.4cm) squares.

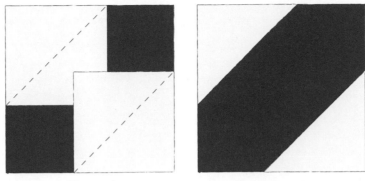

Diagram 1   Diagram 2

Diagram 3

PIECING THE SUB-BLOCKS

Piece together 4 of the red/orange units and 1 blue/green unit into a horizontal row. It does not matter which direction your units face as long as they do not all face the same way. Your finished sub-block should measure 10½" × 2½" (26.7cm × 6.4cm). Diagram 3.

Repeat with the remaining units. You should end up with 320 sub-blocks.

PIECING THE BLOCKS

Piece together 5 sub-blocks into a square. Do your best to match up the seams, though this quilt allows for a lot of wiggle room. Your finished blocks should measure 10½" × 10½" (26.7cm × 26.7cm). Diagram 4.

Repeat for the remaining sub-blocks. You should end up with 64 blocks measuring 10½" × 10½" (26.7cm × 26.7cm).

Diagram 4

PIECING THE TOP

Piece your blocks together in rows of 4. You should end up with 16 rows 40½" (102.9cm) wide.

Piece your rows together, again matching your seams as best you can, but close enough is good enough with this one, assuming close enough is reasonably close.

Your finished top should measure 40½" × 160½" (102.9cm × 407.7cm). Of course, if you would rather do this as a bed quilt, you can do 8 rows of 8 blocks for a top measuring 80½" × 80½" (204.5cm × 204.5cm).

A note on piecing this quilt: I know I've said it before, but you never can have enough pins. Getting all those seams to match up can be a nightmare, especially when piecing together small, pieced blocks. At the same time, it isn't always vital that every seam fit together perfectly; a lot of designs can handle some misalignment. A bit of mismatching in the right circumstances can actually add texture and a bit of visual syncopation. Precision is frequently what is called for, but technique is just a means to an end; carefully consider just what end result you need.

FINISHING THE QUILT

After your top is completed, layer your backing right side down, your batting and the quilt top right side up. Baste the layers together, and then quilt as desired. I asked Lisa to quilt this project with words from the United States' Violence Against Women Act to speak to the systemic issues of domestic violence; that was just one of many possible choices. In many ways, this seems like a piece that is uniquely suited for quilting with text.

Bind using your preferred method.

Credits: Special thanks to Linda Hauschildt, Maggie Magee, Flaun Cline, Kimberly Weese Munoz, Greta Pipke Minton, Shelly Kamp and the Mohawk Valley Quilt Club. Your many hands, along with a handful of others, made it possible to get this one done.

EMBEDDING IDEAS

Some quilts, like *In Defense of Handmade,* need to be bold to assert themselves through direct visual means, but that is not always the case. Subtle, embedded meanings can be every bit as powerful as a literal vocabulary. Forms can take on symbolic meanings and speak through quiet importance. At times, even the most direct elements work best when hidden, only revealing themselves in fragments. So much of the quilting tradition is steeped in visual metaphors; one of the essential questions facing modern quilting is just how we construct a symbolic aesthetic space that speaks uniquely about this time.

4 THE QUILTING TRADITION

Since the day I sat down at my sewing machine to start my first quilt—admittedly with barely a clue as to what I was doing—I have been considering how my practice fits within the quilting tradition, which areas of the tradition I want to draw upon and what possibly new conversations I hope to add. That is the nature of participating in a living tradition, one that is growing and changing even as it seeks to preserve its past. For me, the essential beauty of quilts has a lot to do with the dual pull of historical roots and new developments and the consequent entanglement of past and future in any given quilt.

At the same time, the words *tradition* and *traditional* have become remarkably complicated, much as the word *modern* has. In some spheres, the word *traditional* has been largely associated with the historicist impulse of preserving historic patterns and designs. In some cases, this is true, but that facet has led to an inadvertent perception of quilting as old-fashioned, the impression that the practice of traditional quiltmaking is fundamentally backward looking.

Luckily this impression is not, in fact, the case; quilting is, and always has been, a rich and complicated practice both aesthetically and conceptually. That is why I am rather uncomfortable with the term *traditional*. I prefer the notion of the quilting tradition; I feel like it speaks to an open, expansive practice that perpetually reinvents itself. So much of the quilting tradition, when examined in historical and cultural context, is far from traditional; over the decades and centuries, quilting has been an enormously progressive practice.

My goal for the quilts in this section is to explore my relationship to the quilting tradition; each of these quilts is the result of an active dialogue with various historical practices and motifs. They represent conversations between diverse elements of the quilting tradition, trying to make sense of how it all fits together. These quilts draw upon the past to ask questions about the practice today, to examine how a twenty-first century practice fits within the historical context of quilting and, simultaneously, to explore the unique relevance of that historical practice for current practitioners.

TIMELINE

Everything we do as quilters is interconnected. Whether those connections be small or large, explicit or implicit, we are all working within the same heritage. That said, traditions are constantly changing and evolving, responding to new influences and impulses; a vital practice is perpetually remaking itself anew.

Timeline pays homage to both the tradition of quilting and its continued evolution. The design of *Timeline* traces an overall trajectory; the movement through space is a metaphor for a development over time, but it is a path that can go both ways, forward and backward. As such, its movement does not necessarily connote improvement; instead it recognizes and celebrates change as an expansion of vocabulary that adds to tradition.

It also presents a history in which elements do not directly touch; each step is a leap, a jump from one point to another, rather than a seamless, continual evolution. *Timeline* draws inspiration from Michel Foucault's concept of genealogy from his essay "Nietzsche, Genealogy, History." In it, he says we must look past the general "to identify the accidents, the minute deviations—or conversely, the complete reversals—the errors, the false appraisals, and the faulty calculations that gave birth to those things that continue to exist and have value for us." While the overall design depicts a general path, the individual steps themselves are of greater importance, forming, as they do, the discrete elements that enable the idea of a totality.

The fabrics I have chosen for *Timeline* sketch out a path from the early nineteenth century (in reproduction fabrics) to the leading edge of current quilting fabrics; it posits influences and connections, but only describes one possible path, one historical interpretation. It was laid out dozens of times, each version presenting an alternate history, a different story, some personal and others more academic. Each fabric choice in *Timeline* reshapes the history it records; whether it speaks to the history of quilting or to an individual's quilting history depends entirely on the maker.

FINISHED SIZE

61½" × 81" (156.2cm × 205.7cm)

MATERIALS LIST

- 2 yards (1.8m) solid fabric for right side

- 1 yard (1m) solid fabric for left side

- 1½ yards (1.4m) solid fabric for tween section

- Fat eighths (27.9cm × 45.7cm) of 22 different prints. That will be more than enough, but it will allow room for fussy cutting as desired.

- 5 yards (4.6m) fabric for backing

- ½ yard (0.5m) fabric for binding

- The usual stuff you need to make a quilt (see page 14)

NOTE: This quilt uses three different solids (I used red) that are very closely related, though the visual effect is that there are only two colors. Get the colors as close to each other as possible. For this quilt, I went with Kona Solids because there are so many similar colors to choose from.

The solids you will need are the left-side color, the right-side color and the go-between color (for the thin stripes on each side and also the piecing that winds between the prints). I refer to the three colors as Left, Right and Tween. The Tween solid should be the color that falls between the other two solids tonally.

CUTTING INSTRUCTIONS

From Right solid:

Cut 10 strips for right side:
31½" × 6½" (80.0cm × 16.5cm)

Cut 1 strip for top of right side:
31½" × 4½" (80.0cm × 11.4cm)

FABRIC	CUT	BLOCK NUMBER	PIECE NUMBER
PRINT 1	1 PIECE: 4½" x 2½" (11.4CM x 6.4CM)	1	9
	1 SQUARE: 2½" x 2½" (6.4CM x 6.4CM)	1	7
PRINT 2	2 PIECES: 4½" x 2½" (11.4CM x 6.4CM)	1	1 AND 3
PRINT 3	1 STRIP: 10½" x 2½" (26.7CM x 6.4CM)	1	12
	1 PIECE: 4½" x 2½" (11.4CM x 6.4CM)	1	24
	1 SQUARE: 2½" x 2½" (6.4CM x 6.4CM)	1	14
PRINT 4	3 PIECES: 4½" x 2½" (11.4CM x 6.4CM)	1	15, 17 AND 18
PRINT 5	2 PIECES: 4½" x 2½" (11.4CM x 6.4CM)	1	27 AND 28
PRINT 6	1 STRIP: 10½" x 2½" (26.7CM x 6.4CM)	1	22
	1 PIECE: 4½" x 2½" (11.4CM x 6.4CM)	1	32
	1 SQUARE: 2½" x 2½" (6.4CM x 6.4CM)	1	30
PRINT 7	1 PIECE: 6½" x 2½" (16.5CM x 6.4CM)	1	34
	1 PIECE: 4½" x 2½" (11.4CM x 6.4CM)	2	9
	1 SQUARE: 2½" x 2½" (6.4CM x 6.4CM)	2	7
PRINT 8	2 PIECES: 4½" x 2½" (11.4CM x 6.4CM)	2	1 AND 3
PRINT 9	1 STRIP: 10½" x 2½" (26.7CM x 6.4CM)	2	12
	1 PIECE: 4½" x 2½" (11.4CM x 6.4CM)	2	24
	1 SQUARE: 2½" x 2½" (6.4CM x 6.4CM)	2	14
PRINT 10	3 PIECES: 4½" x 2½" (11.4CM x 6.4CM)	2	15, 17 AND 18
PRINT 11	2 PIECES: 4½" x 2½" (11.4CM x 6.4CM)	2	27 AND 28
PRINT 12	1 STRIP: 10½" x 2½" (26.7CM x 6.4CM)	2	22
	1 PIECE: 4½" x 2½" (11.4CM x 6.4CM)	2	32
	1 SQUARE: 2½" x 2½" (6.4CM x 6.4CM)	2	30
PRINT 13	1 PIECE: 6½" x 2½" (16.5CM x 6.4CM)	2	34
	1 PIECE: 4½" x 2½" (11.4CM x 6.4CM)	3	9
	1 SQUARE: 2½" x 2½" (6.4CM x 6.4CM)	3	7
PRINT 14	2 PIECES: 4½" x 2½" (11.4CM x 6.4CM)	3	1 AND 3

From Left solid:

Cut 10 strips for left side:
17½" × 6½" (44.5cm × 16.5cm)

Cut 1 strip for bottom of left side:
17½" × 4½"(44.5cm × 11.4cm)

From Tween solid:

Cut 11 strips for right side:
31½" × 2½" (80.0cm × 6.4cm)

Cut 11 strips for left side:
17½" × 2½" (44.5cm × 6.4cm)

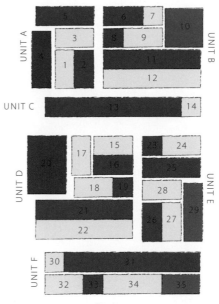

Diagram 1

CUTTING AND PIECING THE BLOCKS

Refer to the chart below for cutting the prints and the solids for the blocks. Number the pieces as shown on the chart.

FABRIC	CUT	BLOCK NUMBER	PIECE NUMBER
PRINT 15	1 STRIP: 10½" x 2½" (26.7CM x 6.4CM) 3		12
	1 PIECE: 4½" x 2½" (11.4CM x 6.4CM) 3		24
	1 SQUARE: 2½" x 2½" (6.4CM x 6.4CM) 3		14
PRINT 16	3 PIECES: 4½" x 2½" (11.4CM x 6.4CM) 3		. . . . .15, 17 AND 18
PRINT 17	2 PIECES: 4½" x 2½" (11.4CM x 6.4CM) 3		. . . . .27 AND 28
PRINT 18	1 STRIP: 10½" x 2½" (26.7CM x 6.4CM) 3		22
	1 PIECE: 4½" x 2½" (11.4CM x 6.4CM) 3		32
	1 SQUARE: 2½" x 2½" (6.4CM x 6.4CM) 3		30
PRINT 19	1 PIECE: 6½" x 2½" (16.5CM x 6.4CM) 3		34
	1 PIECE: 4½" x 2½" (11.4CM x 6.4CM) 4		9
	1 SQUARE: 2½" x 2½" (6.4CM x 6.4CM) 4		7
PRINT 20	2 PIECES: 4½" x 2½" (11.4CM x 6.4CM) 4		. . . . .1 AND 3
PRINT 21	1 STRIP: 10½" x 2½" (26.7CM x 6.4CM) 4		12
	1 PIECE: 4½" x 2½" (11.4CM x 6.4CM) 4		24
	1 SQUARE: 2½" x 2½" (6.4CM x 6.4CM) 4		14
PRINT 22	2 PIECES: 4½" x 2½" (11.4CM x 6.4CM) 4		. . . . .15 AND 17
RIGHT SOLID	4 SQUARES: 4½" x 4½" (11.4CM x 11.4CM) . . . . .1, 2, 3 AND 4		10
	3 PIECES: 6½" x 2½" (16.5CM x 6.4CM) . . . . .1, 2 AND 3		29
	3 PIECES: 4½" x 2½" (11.4CM x 6.4CM) . . . . .1, 2 AND 3		35
LEFT SOLID	4 PIECES: 6½" x 2½" (16.5CM x 6.4CM) . . . . .1, 2, 3 AND 4		4
	3 PIECES: 6½" x 4½" (16.5CM x 11.4CM) . . . . .1, 2 AND 3		20
	1 SQUARE: 4½" x 4½" (11.4CM x 11.4CM) 4		. . . . .20 (PARTIAL)
TWEEN SOLID	14 SQUARES: 2½" x 2½" (6.4CM x 6.4CM) . . . . .1, 2, 3 AND 4		. . . . .8, 23 AND 19, 33 (1, 2 AND 3 ONLY)
	14 PIECES: 4½" x 2½" (11.4CM x 6.4CM) . . . . .1, 2, 3 AND 4		. . . . .2, 6, 16 AND 26 (1, 2 AND 3 ONLY)
	7 PIECES: 6½" x 2½" (16.5CM x 6.4CM) . . . . .1, 2, 3 AND 4		. . . . .5 AND 25 (1, 2 AND 3 ONLY)
	7 STRIPS: 10½" x 2½" (26.7CM x 6.4CM) . . . . .1, 2, 3 AND 4		. . . . .11 AND 21 (1, 2 AND 3 ONLY)
	7 STRIPS: 14½" x 2½" (36.8CM x 6.4CM) . . . . .1, 2, 3 AND 4		. . . . .13 AND 31 (1, 2 AND 3 ONLY)

Piece the four blocks. Elements in the diagram that are shown as touching should be pieced together before being added to the rest of the sub-unit. Diagram 1.

Once all of the sub-units are assembled, piece your sub-units together in order: A + B, and then add C. Sew D + E, and then add F. Then piece A/B/C to D/E/F to complete the block.

Repeat for three full blocks. For the fourth block, assemble units A/B/C and parts of D and E for a partial block.

Sew your blocks together into a single column, making sure they are in the proper order. Diagram 2.

PIECING THE SIDES

Piece together the strips for the right side of the quilt. Begin with the 4½" × 31½" (11.4cm × 80.0cm) strip of the Right solid and then alternate the 2½" × 31½" (6.4cm × 80.0cm) Tween with the 6½" × 31½" (16.5cm × 80.0cm) Right solid strips. Diagram 2.

Piece together the strips for the left side of the quilt. Begin with a Tween strip 2½"× 17½"(6.4cm × 44.5cm) long and alternate with the 6½" × 17½" (16.5cm × 44.5cm) Left solid strips. End the left-side panel with the 4½" × 17½" (11.4cm × 44.5cm) Left solid strip. Diagram 2.

ASSEMBLING THE TOP

First attach the left column to the block column, making sure to carefully match your seams. I suggest using plenty of pins.

Then attach the right column on the other side of the block column, again being careful to match up all of your seams precisely.

FINISHING THE QUILT

After your top is completed, layer your backing right side down, your batting and the quilt top right side up. Baste the layers together, and then quilt as desired. For this quilt, Lisa and I decided on straight lines for the quilting to emphasize a certain rigid or standard unit of time against which the entanglement of the prints could then stand out.

Bind using your preferred method.

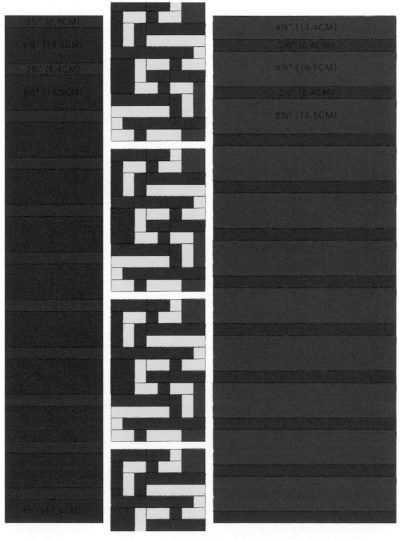

Diagram 2

SPLIT PERSONALITY

This quilt began, at least conceptually, after meeting Jo Morton back in 2011. We were at a dinner together, and it was apparent that we are very different designers; we make for different reasons and utilize distinct vocabularies. In a lot of ways, we work at opposite ends of the quilting spectrum. At the same time, amidst all the apparent contrasts and seeming incompatibilities, we found some common threads, a few core beliefs that spoke through both of our practices. Our differences did not erode and disappear, but we found that our differences were not what defined us.

Split Personality is a quilt built on the notion of commonality in difference. Rather than attempting to erase the differences in style between the two halves of the quilt, it revels in their counterpoints. Instead of seeking an in-between position, the quilt demonstrates that radical differences can function side by side. The Reproduction patchwork and the vast Minimalist space find a balance together; they push and pull against each other, forming a harmonious tension. In the end, the elements serve to reinforce rather than contradict one another.

The essential point of *Split Personality* is that in embracing differences we frequently find relationships—aesthetic, conceptual and personal— that we might never have expected. It speaks to the contrasts between and within us all. *Split Personality* resists homogenization and reduction in favor of a space in which our commonalities are seen through our differences, not despite them. Instead of viewing different styles and approaches as opposite sides of the same coin, it points toward the many coins that may commingle in the same change purse—toward a multiplicity of styles whose differences don't have to be oppositional.

FINISHED SIZE

79" × 77" (200.7cm × 195.6cm)

MATERIALS LIST

- 7 fat quarters (45.7cm × 55.9cm) assorted off-white/cream prints

- 3 fat quarters (45.7cm × 55.9cm) assorted red prints

- 2 fat quarters (45.7cm × 55.9cm) each orange, yellow, green and blue prints

- 2¼ yards (2.1m) purple or other contrasting solid

- 7⅛ yards (6.5m) fabric for backing

- ½ yard (0.5m) fabric for binding

- The usual stuff you need to make a quilt (see page 14)

NOTE: The quantities for the prints are the minimum for doing this quilt. Feel free to play with as many prints as you like; the more, the better. And really, you can do this quilt with any color arrangement.

CUTTING INSTRUCTIONS

Prints:

Cut 356 squares from off-white/cream prints: 2½" × 2½" (6.4cm × 6.4cm)

Cut 114 squares from red prints: 2½" × 2½" (6.4cm × 6.4cm)

Cut 26 squares from orange prints: 2½" × 2½" (6.4cm × 6.4cm)

Cut 97 squares from yellow prints: 2½"× 2½" (6.4cm × 6.4cm)

Cut 106 squares from green prints: 2½" × 2½"(6.4cm × 6.4cm)

Cut 97 squares from blue prints: 2½" × 2½" (6.4cm × 6.4cm)

Contrasting solid:

Cut 1 piece: 50½" × 38½" (128.3cm × 97.8cm)

Cut 1 piece: 16½" × 38½" (41.9cm × 97.8cm)

Cut 1 square: 16½" × 16½" (41.9cm × 41.9cm)

Cut 1 piece: 8½" × 16½" (21.6cm × 41.9cm)

Cut 6 strips: 14½" × 2½" (36.8cm × 6.4cm)

Cut 5 strips: 10½" × 2½" (26.7cm × 6.4cm)

Cut 9 strips: 6½" × 2½" (16.5cm × 6.4cm)

Cut 4 pieces: 4½" × 2½" (11.4cm × 6.4cm)

Cut 4 squares: 2½" × 2½" (6.4cm × 6.4cm)

PIECING THE TOP

Piece together the diamond blocks as shown in the diagrams, making sure that the colors that cross from one block to another match up. Each of the 15 diamond blocks is 6 squares wide by 8 squares long. Diagram 1, Unit A.

Piece together 3 rows of 6 squares each; these are Unit B in Diagram 1. Piece together a row of 3 squares for Unit C. These rows ensure that the top of the quilt is colorful rather than primarily cream.

Piece together 5 Unit D blocks that integrate the prints and the solids as shown in the diagram. Each Unit D block uses a 14½" × 2½" (36.8cm × 6.4cm) strip, a 10½" × 2½" (26.7cm × 6.4cm) strip and a 6½" × 2½" (16.5cm × 6.4cm) strip of the solid fabric.

Sew three Unit A blocks and 1 Unit D block to form a row. Repeat to create a total of 5 rows. Do not sew those rows together yet; you are going to piece the quilt in horizontal groups to be sure that the diamond in the solid side lines up perfectly.

Piece the Unit E diamond for the contrast solid side as shown in the diagram. You should use up the remaining print squares and your remaining purple strips.

UNIT E

Diagram 2

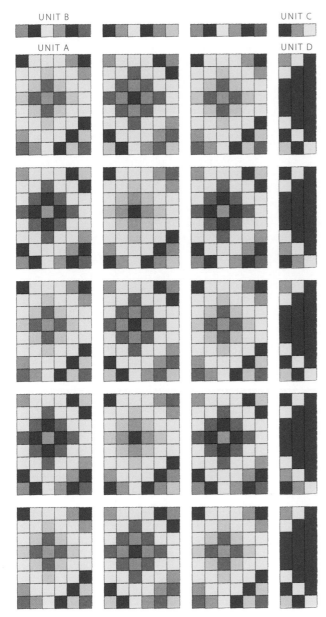

UNIT B

UNIT A

UNIT C

UNIT D

Diagram 1

BEYOND SYMMETRY

Balance and symmetry are very different things; in fact, symmetry is often rather unbalanced. Think of a spinning top. It may well be perfectly symmetrical, but only tenuously so; it is perpetually on the edge of wavering and toppling over. So much of Modern design has been an exploration of the ways in which asymmetrical tensions can come together to produce remarkable harmonies. Consider Constructivism, the Bauhaus and Swiss Modernism; each of these—and many more—engaged different models for examining the complex relationship between harmony and tension. When laying out a quilt, consider ways in which you can use elements to counterbalance each other within the space. A little bit of play might just result in a quilt that is both more engaging and more harmonious.

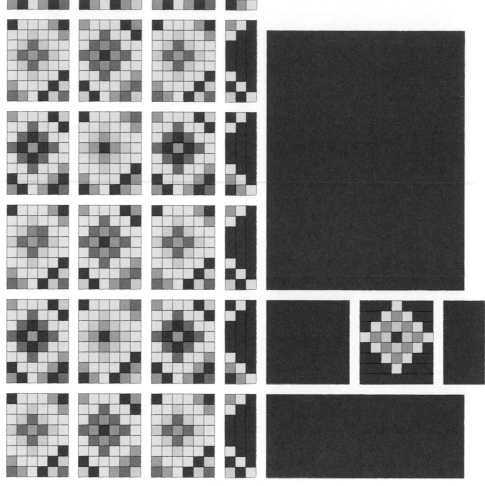

Diagram 3

Sew the 16½" (41.9cm) square to the left side of the diamond and then the 8½" × 16½" (21.6cm × 41.9cm) rectangle to the right side of the diamond. Diagram 3.

Sew the 3 Unit B rows to Unit C to make one long row. Sew this row to the top of one A/D row. Then sew this row to 2 more A/D rows. Sew the right side of the 50½" × 38½" (128.3cm × 97.8cm) solid fabric to this section.

Sew the fourth row of A/D blocks to the row with the solid fabric and inset diamond.

Sew the bottom row of blocks to the 16½" × 38½" (41.9cm × 97.8cm) piece of solid fabric.

Piece the 3 groups together, making sure they are in the proper order.

FINISHING THE QUILT

After your top is completed, layer your backing right side down, your batting and the quilt top right side up. Baste the layers together, and then quilt as desired. I actually stunned Lisa by asking her to do feathers for this quilt, at least on the "traditional" sections. We worked together to develop a strategy that would both emphasize the different aspects of the quilt while still serving to unify the quilt.

Bind using your preferred method. For this quilt, I used two fabrics for my binding. I made the binding strip with an equal length of each fabric, then I carefully pinned the binding in place, matching the binding fabrics to the top fabrics, before sewing it down.

Credits: This top was pieced by Audrie Bidwell.

This quilt was pieced using prints by Jo Morton for Andover Fabrics and Kona Solid in Berry from Robert Kaufman.

CINDERBLOCK

*C*inderblock is perhaps the most straightforward quilt in the entire book; it is fundamentally a response to Log Cabin blocks. Now don't get me wrong; I love Log Cabin blocks. They are enormously flexible and variable. Let's be blunt: they're kind of awesome. At the same time, they are definitively a nineteenth century reference; in the twenty-first century, log cabins are more a vanity than a necessity.

Much in the same way that Log Cabin blocks take their inspiration from the way actual log cabins are constructed, *Cinderblock* is a tribute of sorts to an essential modern building material: the cinder block. Taking that ubiquitous form as a starting point, the goal was to find a way to transform that essential shape into a space for color and play, much like a Log Cabin block. The quilt pays specific homage to the basic conceptual practices that underpin the quilting tradition, even as it takes its inspiration from an explicitly modern material, channeling the essence of quilting as a richly symbolic activity.

The interplay of inner and outer shapes becomes a vehicle for color exploration, converting the drab monotony of stacked cinder blocks into a riot of vibrant hues. Just as Log Cabin quilts invite the use of diverse fabrics, colors and styles, *Cinderblock* offers the potential for enormous contrast or quiet subtlety both within individual blocks and between them.

FINISHED SIZE

64" x 82" (162.6cm x 208.3cm)

MATERIALS LIST

- ³⁄₈ yard (0.3m) each of 2 different tones of deep red, 2 different tones of deep orange, 2 different tones of deep yellow, 2 different tones of deep green, 2 different tones of deep blue and 2 different tones of deep purple

- ¼ yard (0.2m) each of 2 different tones of pale red, 2 different tones of pale orange, 2 different tones of pale yellow, 2 different tones of pale green, 2 different tones of pale blue and 2 different tones of pale purple

- ¼ yard (0.2m) gray fabric

- 5 yards (4.6m) fabric for backing

- ½ yard (0.5m) fabric for binding

- The usual stuff you need to make a quilt (see page 14)

NOTE: To make this quilt as pictured, make sure you note which of the different tones goes in which place, though in reality it doesn't matter. The multiple tones of both the inner and outer colors are just to add more vibrancy and variation to the quilt, so you need not follow any particular order. Just make sure you don't split a single block into two distinctly different colors.

CUTTING INSTRUCTIONS

Block Unit A (Left side)

From 1 deep red, 1 deep orange, 1 deep yellow, 1 deep green, 1 deep blue and 1 deep purple:

    Cut 4 squares: 4½" × 4½" (11.4cm × 11.4cm)

    Cut 2 strips: 6½" × 2½" (16.5cm × 6.4cm)

    Cut 2 strips: 8½" × 2½" (21.6cm × 6.4cm)

From 1 pale red, 1 pale orange, 1 pale yellow, 1 pale green, 1 pale blue and 1 pale purple:

    Cut 4 squares: 2½" × 2½" (6.4cm × 6.4cm)

    Cut 2 strips: 6½" × 2½" (16.5cm × 6.4cm)

    Cut 2 strips: 8½" × 2½" (21.6cm × 6.4cm)

    Cut 1 strip: 8½" × 6½" (21.6cm × 16.5cm)

Block Unit B (Right side)

From remaining deep red, deep orange, deep yellow, deep green, deep blue and deep purple:

    Cut 4 squares: 4½" × 4½" (11.4cm × 11.4cm)

    Cut 1 strip: 6½" × 2½" (16.5cm × 6.4cm)

    Cut 1 strip: 6½" × 1½" (16.5cm × 3.8cm)

    Cut 2 strips: 8½" × 2½" (21.6cm × 6.4cm)

From remaining pale red, pale orange, pale yellow, pale green, pale blue and pale purple:

    Cut 4 squares: 2½" × 2½" (6.4cm × 6.4cm)

    Cut 2 strips: 6½" × 2½" (16.5cm × 6.4cm)

    Cut 2 strips: 8½" × 2½" (21.6cm × 6.4cm)

    Cut 1 strip: 8½" × 6½" (21.6cm × 16.5cm)

From gray, cut 12 strips:
6½" × 1½" (16.5cm × 3.8cm)

All Block Units

Cut the curves for the 4½" × 4½" (11.4cm × 11.4cm) outer pieces and the curves for the 2½" × 2½" (6.4cm × 6.4cm) inner pieces using the templates on page 117.

PIECING THE QUILT BLOCKS

For each Block Unit A, piece the four deep-colored 4½" × 4½" (11.4cm × 11.4cm) curved corner pieces to the four pale-colored 2½" × 2½" (6.4cm × 6.4cm) curved corner pieces.

Piece the two deep 6½" × 2½" (16.5cm × 6.4cm) strips to the corresponding pale strips. Piece the two deep 8½" × 2½" (21.6cm × 6.4cm) to the corresponding pale strips.

Piece together each block in three columns. Diagram 1.

1. Top-left corner, left side, bottom-left corner

2. Top side, large center rectangle, bottom side

3. Top-right corner, right side, bottom-right corner

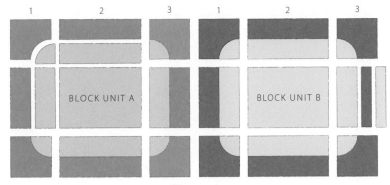

Diagram 1

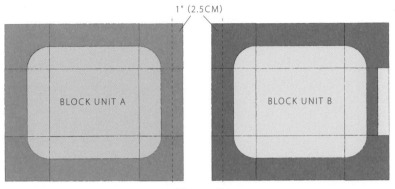

Diagram 2

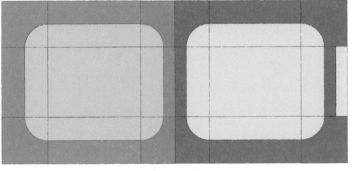

Diagram 3

Piece together the three columns, making sure all seams match up. The block unit should measure 16½" × 14½" (41.9cm × 36.8cm). Trim one short side so the block measures 15½" × 14½" (39.4cm × 36.8cm). Diagram 2.

For each Block Unit B, repeat the instructions on page 108 for piecing the curved pieces.

Piece the deep-colored 6½" × 1½" (16.5cm × 3.8cm) strip to the gray strip of the same size.

Piece the sides and columns as described above, except place the deep color/gray strip on the right side of the block, with the gray on the outer edge.

The block unit should measure 16½" × 14½" (41.9cm × 36.8cm). Trim the left short side so the block measures 15½" × 14½" (39.4cm × 36.8cm). Diagram 2.

Sew together the trimmed side of a Block Unit A to the trimmed side of a Block Unit B. The final block should measure 30½" × 14½" (77.5cm × 36.8cm). Diagram 3.

ASSEMBLING THE QUILT

Make as many blocks and partial blocks as necessary for the quilt. For this quilt, I made 6 full blocks and 12 partial blocks. All partial blocks are composed of either one or two columns from Unit Block A or Unit Block B (see page 109).

Note: The rows with the large partial blocks will be 2" (5.1cm) wider than the rows with the small partial blocks. You can either trim these evenly from each side or all from one side, depending on your preference.

Assemble all of your rows, and then piece together your rows to complete the top.

ON COLOR

Over the years, there have been a million and one different color rules, systems and tricks, and all of them are wrong. Well, not necessarily wrong, but narrow and incomplete. The problem is that all of the rules and systems are general; they are guidelines, and as such, they tend toward the universal. On the other hand, every use of color is specific, involving unique proportions, tones and relationships. All of those details matter and do more to guide what colors may or may not work than any system ever could.

My rule of thumb is that every color can indeed go with every other color. Figuring out what, in fact, works is what experiments and play are for. When in doubt, go overboard, and then pull it back. The only way to find that fine line between awesome and awful is to cross it; otherwise, you never can be quite sure just where it is. The real key is figuring out what you want your colors to do, to speak to; only then will you have a basis on which to make decisions. Color is just a means to getting to an idea, even if that idea is simply to play with a whole lot of color.

FINISHING THE QUILT

After your top is completed, layer your backing right side down, your batting and the quilt top right side up. Baste the layers together, and then quilt as desired. For this quilt, Lisa contrasted the dense building-block feel for the outer shapes of the cinder blocks against the straight lines of the interior, negative spaces, reinforcing the fundamental interplay of the blocks themselves.

Bind using your preferred method.

AFTERWORD

After writing this book and completing all of these quilts, I find that I keep returning to a single phrase: Go Make Stuff. In many ways, that encapsulates everything I believe about modern quilting. Making stuff has very little to do with being modern or traditional, or with questions of whether something is good or bad. Instead, I keep returning to the practice of sitting down and making, just as one might keep a journal—the ideal of allowing one's quilting practice to reflect the immediacy of one's life.

Each of these quilts comes directly from my experience, the way I think about and look at the world. I sincerely hope that these quilts speak to you and offer ways of talking about your own life and perspectives. Each quilt is a template of sorts: it lays out a road map, but the myriad minute decisions—the fabrics, the colors, the quilting and the underlying reasons for each of those choices—that go into each new making will truly bring the quilt to life.

On another level, though, I hope that these quilts and the words that surround them will offer a road map of another sort, to a perspective on a quilting practice. Many of the quilts in this book tackle big issues and grand themes: from domestic violence and same-sex marriage to the nature of community and the idea of history itself. As an academic, the large ideas always appeal to me, but not every idea has to be monumental. The small idea can be every bit as vital as the large; significance is not born of scale.

This simple quilt may be the most important quilt I have made. It does not speak of politics or society directly; it speaks of my daughter. One day my then three-year-old daughter and I were holding hands while walking to the coffee shop down the street. Abruptly, she stopped and pointed at the shadow we cast upon the sidewalk and proclaimed rather excitedly, "We are an *H*, Papa!" Not only do I love that she had started using shadows to form letters, but I simply adore the way she phrased it. We didn't make an *H*, we *were* an *H*. Hence, this quilt. It is us.

The thing is that the very act of making this quilt is tied to a social and political perspective. The very act of making rather than buying, of imbuing the things in our lives with meaning, is part of a very modern, or more accurately postmodern, perspective. It is a reaction against disposability; it anticipates a longer arc of history, one that includes passing our creations down through generations. While these are very traditional themes in many ways, they have been taken up again by the modern crafting community as a response to a seemingly impersonal social sphere. The ideas are old, but this different context reforms them anew.

No longer are quilts primarily a necessity; they are an explicit response and a reaction to the world we live in. Quilts reflect our joys and sorrows, our emotions and intellect, our solitary acts and extended relations more than any list could fully convey. When each of us heads off to Go Make Stuff, the most immediate question is generally one of what to make. To that I want to add one more word: why? Therein lies the profound resonance that comes with making.

INSTRUCTIONS FOR URNH

MATERIALS LIST

18 different ½ yard (0.5m) prints

5 yards (4.6m) fabric for backing

½ yard (0.5m) fabric for binding

The usual stuff you need to make a quilt (see page 14)

This quilt finishes to 64" × 80" (162.6cm × 203.2cm), perfect for a twin bed. The long arms of the *H*s finish at 4" × 12" (10.2cm × 30.5cm), cut to 4½" × 12½" (11.4cm × 31.8cm). The cross parts of the *H*s finish to 4" (10.2cm) squares, cut to 4½" (11.4cm) squares. At the top and bottom of columns, you will occasionally need to truncate a long arm on an *H* to finish at 8" × 4" (20.3cm × 10.2cm), cut to 8½" × 4½" (21.6cm × 11.4cm).

You can do this with as few or as many different prints as you want. I made mine using 18 different ½ yard (0.5m) cuts, but I wanted the extra variety and am always happy to have extra bits to piece into the back or to make a spare baby quilt. In my book, the more variety, the better for this one.

As far as piecing goes, just piece the columns as they are in the diagram. There need not be any particular pattern to where each print goes, as long as the prints come together properly to form the *H*s.

To make it bigger, just continue the pattern. Each column follows the pattern of long-long-short, and the columns repeat every seven columns. Add more pieces to each column to make them longer (accounting properly for truncated elements at the top or bottom of columns), and add more columns. If you want to make it smaller, you can just stop your columns sooner and do fewer columns. Alternately, you can either shrink or enlarge the size of the elements.

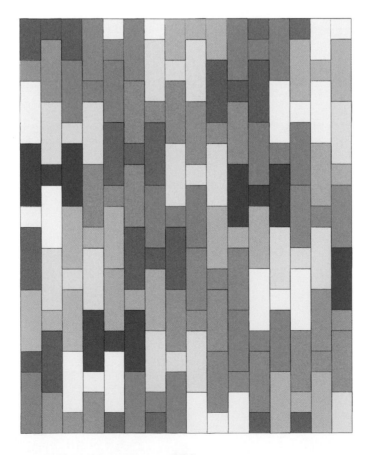

TEMPLATES

These templates are provided for your personal use.
Trace them onto tracing paper or photocopy them to
make templates.

For *Sum of Interrelations*, page 40. Shown here at 100%.

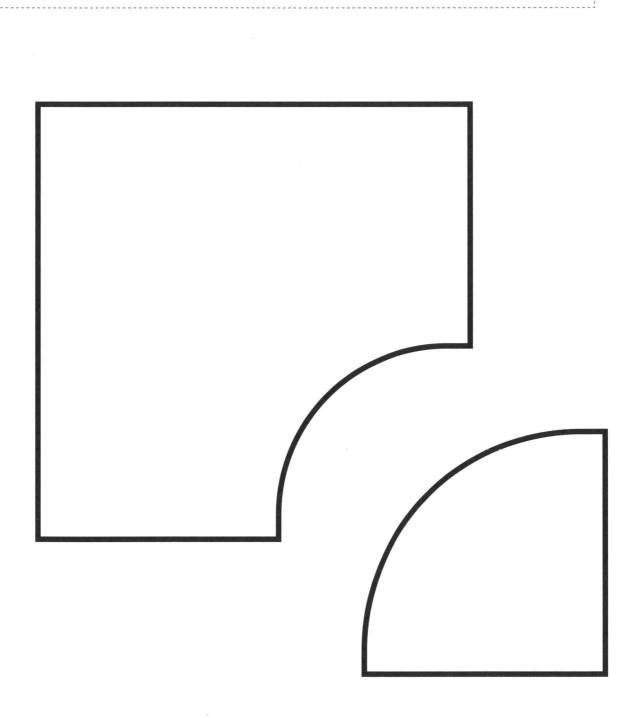

For *Cinderblock*, page 106. Shown here at 100%.

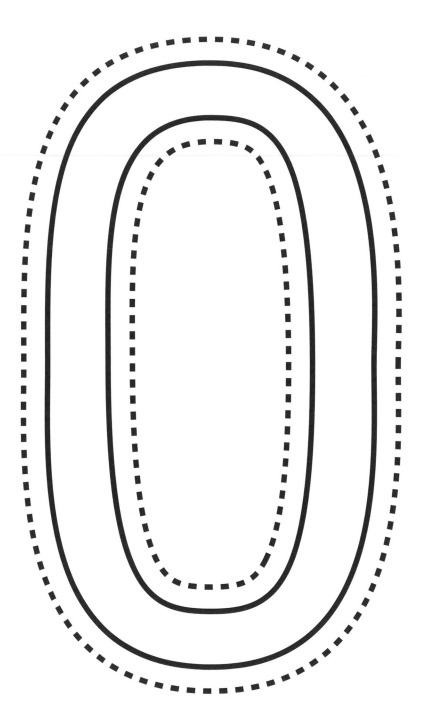

For *In Defense of Handmade*, page 72. Shown here at 100%. The straight line is the cutting line for raw-edge appliqué. The dotted line is the ¼" (6mm) seam allowance for turned appliqué.

For *In Defense of Handmade,* page 72. Shown here at 100%. The straight line is the cutting line for raw-edge appliqué. The dotted line is the ¼" (6mm) seam allowance for turned appliqué.

For *In Defense of Handmade*, page 72. Shown here at 100%. The straight line is the cutting line for raw-edge appliqué. The dotted line is the ¼" (6mm) seam allowance for turned appliqué.

For *In Defense of Handmade*, page 72. Shown here at 100%. The straight line is the cutting line for raw-edge appliqué. The dotted line is the ¼" (6mm) seam allowance for turned appliqué.

For *In Defense of Handmade,* page 72. Shown here at 100%. The straight line is the cutting line for raw-edge appliqué. The dotted line is the ¼" (6mm) seam allowance for turned appliqué.

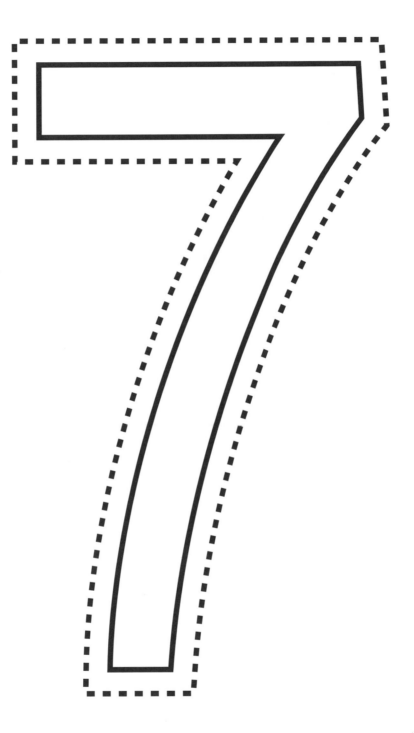

For *In Defense of Handmade*, page 72. Shown here at 100%. The straight line is the cutting line for raw-edge appliqué. The dotted line is the ¼" (6mm) seam allowance for turned appliqué.

RESOURCES

The materials used to make the projects in this book can be found at your local quilt shop or fabric store. For information about specific products, please contact the manufacturers listed below.

Andover Fabrics
andoverfabrics.com

Birch Fabrics
www.birchfabrics.com

FreeSpirit Fabrics
www.freespiritfabric.com

Liberty of London
www.liberty.co.uk

Michael Miller Fabrics
michaelmillerfabrics.com

Moda Fabrics
www.unitednotions.com

Pellon
www.pellonprojects.com

Robert Kaufman Fabrics
www.robertkaufman.com

INDEX

¼" (6mm) foot 16, 23

Ampersand 28–33

Answer Key 34–39

appliqué foot 16

appliqué

    raw edge 22–23

    reverse 37

backs of quilts 23–24

batting 15

binding 25

books, as resource 19

buttoned quilts 62–69

buttons and loops, attaching 66-67

camera, as tool 17

Cinderblock 106–111

clear ruler 16

collaborative quilt 40

color choice 110

curves, piecing 21

cutting long strips 20

cutting mat 14

design wall 16

Double Edged Love 8

Double Wedding Ring 80

Excess 86–91

fabric 18

    prints vs. solids 58

    single collections 68

    timeline 94

    tonal variation 30

fusible web 16

glue stick 15

half-square triangles 53

    technique 52

hand sewing needle 14

handmade, what is 72, 74

ideas, embedding 91

In Defense of Handmade 8, 72–79

inspiration 64

Internet

    as community 27, 40

    as resource 19

    as tool 16

iron 16

labels, quilt 24–25, 46

library card, as tool 17

marking pen 16

memorial quilts 86

Mitosis 56–61

modern quilting 8, 11–12, 53, 88, 93, 103, 112

museums, as resource 19

needle

    hand sewing 14

    machine sewing 15

Palimpsest (Pride Flag) 80–85

palimpsest 80

piecing curves 21

pinning 21, 76

pins 14

quilt guild, as resource 19

quilts

    backs 23–24

    collaborative 40, 45

    labels 24–25, 46

    memorial 86

    purpose of 11, 32, 45, 49, 71, 112

    political 82

    story 28

quilting, *see also* modern quilting, traditional quilting

    community 27, 71

    as craft 13

    modern vs. traditional 93

    technique 25, 60, 80

    tradition 93, 94, 106

Morton, Jo 100

newspapers, as resource 19

randomness 42

raw edge appliqué 22–¬23

Reunion 62–69

reverse appliqué 37

"Room of One's Own" 17

rotary cutter 14

scissors 15

seam allowance 23

seam ripper 16

sewing machine feed 16

sewing machine needle 15

Sipes, Lisa 25, 30, 38, 54, 60, 66, 78, 90, 98, 104, 110

social media

    as tool 16

    as resource 19

Split Personality 100–105

sticky notes, as tool 16

story quilt 28

Sum of Interrelations 40–47

symmetry 103

table runner 34–39

tape measure 16

thread 16

Timeline 94–99

tonal variation 30

traditional quilting 93

trapunto technique 78

tying technique 44

URNH 8, 114–115

walking foot 16

Wolfe, Victoria Findlay 8

Woolf, Virginia 17

You Are Here 50–55

Other fine KP Craft books are available from your favorite bookstore, fabric or craft store or online supplier.

18 17 16 15 14   5 4 3 2 1

www.fwmedia.com

DISTRIBUTED IN CANADA BY FRASER DIRECT
100 Armstrong Avenue
Georgetown, ON, Canada L7G 5S4
Tel: (905) 877-4411

DISTRIBUTED IN THE U.K. AND EUROPE
by F&W Media International LTD
Brunel House, Forde Close Newton Abbot, Devon TQ12 4PU, UK
Tel: (+44) 1626 323200, Fax: (+44) 1626 323319
Email: enquiries@fwmedia.com

DISTRIBUTED IN AUSTRALIA BY CAPRICORN LINK
P.O. Box 704, S. Windsor NSW, 2756 Australia
Tel: (02) 4577-3555

Edited by Christine Doyle
Designed by Julie Barnett
Photography by John Carrico, Alias Imaging; Mary Hautman, Alias Imaging; Christine Polomsky
Production coordinated by Greg Nock

METRIC CONVERSION CHART

to convert	to	multiply by
inches	centimeters	2.54
centimeters	inches	0.4
feet	centimeters	30.5
centimeters	feet	0.03
yards	meters	0.9
meters	yards	1.1

ABOUT THE AUTHOR

I am a geek—always have been, always will be. I spent most of my childhood amassing math awards aplenty. Sometime in high school, I grew tired of memorizing formulae and took up art; I couldn't draw or anything, but still it seemed a good idea. I was lucky enough to go to a high school that had a mammoth weaving studio, and there the combination of math, aesthetics and concepts just clicked. I decided to see if I could logic my way into art and have been trying to do that ever since.

During my undergraduate studies at Kenyon College, my practice shifted heavily to sculpture, though weaving and sewing remained recurrent motifs in the things I made. As I moved on to do graduate degrees at Ohio University and the Cranbrook Academy of Art, the ideas of stitching contrasting concepts and forms together—both literally and figuratively—permeated my work, whether it was physical objects or programming-based multimedia projects.

After teaching design at Drake University, I moved to upstate New York to start a family and continue my academic career, but I soon fell ill with a rare form of muscular dystrophy known as hypokalemic periodic paralysis. Two years later, we finally found an effective management protocol, and I began sewing for my young daughter. I instantly fell in love with the practice and began designing fabric and sewing quilts. From there it has been a remarkable rollercoaster ride, one wonderfully filled with fabric, quilts and an extraordinary community. Oh, and more quilts. Always more quilts...

MORE MODERN QUILTS YOU CAN MAKE!

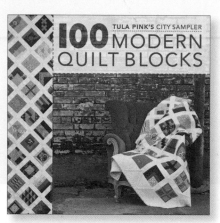

Tula Pink's City Sampler

By Tula Pink

Quilt along with Tula Pink to make 100 modern, city-inspired quilt blocks. Then use them to make any of the three quilts in the book, or make up your very own setting. A variety of fabrics and Tula's amazing eye for color combinations will make all of the blocks and quilts pop off the page. Beautiful illustrations and photography will entice quilters of all levels to make their own City Sampler Quilt.

Quilts from the House of Tula Pink

By Tula Pink

Welcome to the world of cutting-edge fabric designer, Tula Pink, where clever quilts show off fanciful fabric, and your imagination can be let out to play. Featuring fabrics that you know and love, Tula offers 20 patterns with her signature flair for color, design and original style. Between 10 amazing quilts and 10 extra-cool companion projects, you'll be inspired to play with fabric, color and design in a way like never before!

Modern Designs for Classic Quilts

By Kelly Biscopink and Andrea Johnson

Learn to create the traditional quilt blocks you love in a way that reflects your own unique style! The twelve classic quilt blocks and designs in this book are all made with a fresh twist that will appeal to modern quilters who want to take their quilting to the next level and to traditional quilters who want to embrace a modern aesthetic. Includes twelve quilts and seven smaller projects.